COURAGE TO CHANGE

The Christian Roots of the Twelve-Step Movement

Compiled and edited by
Bill Pittman with Dick B.

HAZELDEN

Hazelden
Center City, Minnesota 55012-0176
1-800-328-9000
http://www.hazelden.org

ISBN: 1-56838-245-6

Unless otherwise noted, Scripture quotations are from the King James
version of the Bible.

Scripture quotations identified Moffatt are from The Bible: A New
Translation by James Moffatt © 1954 by James A. R. Moffatt.
By permission of HarperCollins Publishers, Inc.

Scripture quotations identified NIV are from the HOLY BIBLE, NEW
INTERNATIONAL VERSION®. NIV®. Copyright © 1973, 1978,
1984 by International Bible Society. Used by permission of Zondervan
Publishing House. All rights reserved.

Scripture quotations identified RSV are taken from the Revised Standard
Version of the Bible, copyright 1946, 1952, 1971, and 1973 by the
Division of Christian Education of the National Council of the Churches
of Christ in the United States of America.

The Twelve Steps are reprinted and adapted with permission of Alcoholics
Anonymous World Services, Inc. Permission to reprint or adapt the Twelve
Steps does not mean that Alcoholics Anonymous has reviewed or approved
the contents of the publication, nor that A.A. agrees with the views
expressed herein. The views expressed herein are solely those of the
authors. A.A. is a program of recovery from alcoholism. Use of the Twelve
Steps in connection with programs and activities which are patterned after
A.A., but which address others problems, does not imply otherwise.

COURAGE TO CHANGE

"We A.A.'s think, Sam, that if your only admission ticket to Heaven was a certificate of what you have done for us, then St. Peter would assign you something much better than a bleacher seat right from the start."

—Bill Wilson to Sam
February 27, 1957

Abbreviations used in this book for Shoemaker writings:

CC	*The Conversion of the Church*
CCSW	*The Church Can Save the World*
CF	*Confident Faith*
CSB	*Children of the Second Birth*
GATY	*The Gospel According to You*
GC	*God's Control*
IIBL	*If I Be Lifted Up*
NA	*National Awakening*
RR	*Realizing Religion*
RTW	*Religion That Works*
TBM	*Twice-Born Ministers*
YMV	*A Young Man's View of the Ministry*

Contents

Acknowledgments

People who assisted us with information on Sam Shoemaker: Helen Smith Shoemaker, Sally Shoemaker Robinson, Nickie Shoemaker Haggart, Mrs. W. Irving Harris, Dr. Thomas F. Pike, Rev. Stephen Garmey, James Draper and Eleanor Forde Newton, L. Parks Shipley Sr., James Houck, George Vondermuhll Jr., Rev. T. Willard Hunter, and David Sack.

People who assisted us with information on the Oxford Group: Garth D. Lean, Kenneth D. Belden, Michael Hutchinson, Charles Haines, Rev. Howard Blake, Rev. Harry J. Almond, Richard Ruffin, and Donald Johnson, together with Mrs. Harris, the Newtons, Shipley, Houck, Vondermuhll, and Hunter.

A.A. founding survivors who assisted us: Sue Smith Windows, Robert R. and Elizabeth Smith, Dorothy Williams Culver, John F. Seiberling, Dorothy Seiberling, Mary Seiberling Huhn, and Nell Wing.

A.A. historians: Dr. Ernest Kurtz, Charles Bishop Jr., Mel B., Earl H., Charlie P., Joe McQ., Bob and Fay W., Ray G., Gail L., Paul L., Bruce W., Mitch K., Dennis C., Mary D., Mike K., and Frank M.

Archives and libraries: Dr. Bob's home; Stepping Stones; General Services in New York; Seeley G. Mudd Library at Princeton University; Akron University; Akron Public Library; Princeton Public Library; San Francisco Theological Seminary; Golden Gate Baptist Seminary; Graduate Theological Union; Hartford Seminary; Kahului, Kihei, Makawao, and Wailuku Public Libraries on Maui.

Immense personal assistance: Dick B.'s son, Ken, and our readers—Jack Cawkwell, Lisa Dugan, Hal Durham, Angus Lamont, Peter and Regina LeShane, Linda McClelland, Curtis Monahan, and Bob Morris.

Introduction

The true story of the meeting of two alcoholics at the Seiberling Gate House in Akron, Ohio, on Mother's Day of 1935 has often been told. So too the account of subsequent events which, in little more than fifty years, catapulted a meager recovery group of about a hundred men and women into a world-changing fellowship of more than two million. What have not been told are the details of the spiritual recovery material the two alcoholics heard, learned, and applied. They obtained the material from A First Century Christian Fellowship—founded by a Lutheran minister, Dr. Frank N. D. Buchman and led in New York City by his chief American lieutenant, Rev. Samuel Moor Shoemaker Jr. rector of Calvary Episcopal Church. This fellowship changed its name to the Oxford Group in 1928.

The two alcoholics were the financially ruined New York stockbroker Bill Wilson and the very sick and broke Akron physician Dr. Robert H. Smith. The two, respectively, came to be known as "Bill W." and "Dr. Bob." Prior to their meeting, each had been associated with the Oxford Group.

Bill W.'s association had begun when one of his old drinking friends, Ebby Thatcher, had carried a message of his Oxford Group recovery to Bill in New York. Bill had hustled himself to Calvary Mission, where Ebby had surrendered his life to God. There, in a drunken condition, Bill

11

had made a decision for Christ. Later, he had checked into Towns Hospital to detox. Then—with the help of Ebby—Bill had applied the Oxford Group life-changing technique, surrendered his life to God, and experienced what he later called his "hot flash" religious experience—which freed him for the rest of his life from the obsession to drink. Bill had immediately begun attending Oxford Group meetings at Sam Shoemaker's Calvary House, adjacent to the Calvary Church in New York. Somehow, Bill had learned the Oxford Group principles from Rev. Shoemaker, had started to work with other alcoholics—to no avail—and had finally come to Akron on an ill-fated financial deal, which ultimately led him to his meeting with Dr. Bob.

Dr. Bob's Oxford Group relationship had a different genesis. Some two and a half years before he met Bill, Dr. Bob had been introduced to the Oxford Group as the result of a headline-making visit of Dr. Frank Buchman and a team of thirty Oxford Group workers who had come to Akron at the invitation of Harvey Firestone. Firestone's son, Russell, had sustained a "miraculous" recovery from alcoholism on a train from Denver with the help of one of the Oxford Group leaders, Rev. Sam Shoemaker. Russell's grateful father had invited Oxford Group founder Dr. Frank Buchman and his team to Akron to tell of their program. Henrietta Seiberling, Dr. Bob's wife, Anne, and some others had attended the Oxford Group doings, and they very shortly had had Dr. Bob involved. The Oxford Group members, learning of Dr. Bob's drinking problem, had endeavored to help him by spiritual means. Dr. Bob had studied the Bible, prayed, joined a church, attended Oxford Group meetings, read Oxford Group and other Christian literature, and fellowshipped with the Akron Oxford Group adherents. But he had stayed drunk. Undeterred, the Oxford Group people had joined him in prayers for his recovery. And the prayers were soon answered.

Bill W. showed up in Akron, had a five-hour discussion with Dr. Bob, and carried a recovery message that seemed to have real impact. The versions of what happened differ. But Dr. Bob was clear that he learned from Bill the Oxford Group message of *service*. The two set about feverishly "oxidizing" alcoholics in Akron. Dr. Bob had a brief relapse, but recovered on June 10, 1935–the founding date of A.A.– never to drink again. For the next few years, Dr. Bob worked with alcoholics in Akron, and Bill, with much less success, did likewise in New York. By 1938 some forty people had recovered, and the fellowship determined to write a text describing the steps they took to recover. Their book, *Alcoholics Anonymous,* is affectionately called the "Big Book" because of its large size at the time. That book–containing and explaining A.A.'s suggested Twelve Steps of Recovery– has now had more than ten million copies published. The Big Book is A.A.'s road map and is the source for the recovery ideas of a host of other twelve-step programs today.

Why this book on the writings of Sam Shoemaker? First, because A.A.'s founders–especially Bill W.–indicated that their recovery ideas came from the Bible, the Oxford Group, and particularly Sam Shoemaker. Second, because practically the only word-of-mouth contact between Oxford Group leaders and A.A. was through Sam Shoemaker, his Calvary Church staff, and the Oxford Group leaders in Shoemaker's New York area. Third, because there is a marked resemblance today between the language in A.A.'s Big Book and fellowship and the words of Sam Shoemaker in the many books he wrote between 1923 and 1939, the date A.A.'s Big Book was written. Finally, because the very depth and beauty of Shoemaker's Christian writings may challenge or tempt A.A. members and others interested in the biblical principles of recovery embodied in A.A.'s Twelve Steps to dig out the original Shoemaker books and savor their beauty and force.

Where Bill Wilson Said He Got the Twelve Steps

At A.A.'s twentieth anniversary convention in St. Louis, Bill Wilson brought Rev. Sam Shoemaker to the stage and said:

> I have been wondering how many hours some of us in this room, including me, have spent in criticizing the men of religion. Yet they have taught us all that we know of things spiritual. It is through Sam Shoemaker that most of A.A.'s spiritual principles have come.[1]

In his account of the St. Louis convention, Bill wrote:

> Sam's appearance before us was further evidence that many a channel had been used by Providence to create Alcoholics Anonymous. And none had been more vitally needed than the one opened through Sam Shoemaker and his Oxford Group associates of a generation before. The basic principles which the Oxford Groupers had taught were ancient and universal ones, the common property of mankind . . . the important thing is this: the early A.A. got its ideas of self-examination, acknowledgment of character defects, restitution for harm done, and working with others straight from the Oxford Groups and directly from Sam Shoemaker, their former leader in America, and from nowhere else.[2]

In *The Language of the Heart,* a compilation of Bill's writings in A.A.'s *Grapevine,* Bill is recorded as follows:

> Where did the early A.A.s find the material for the remaining ten Steps? Where did we learn about moral inventory, amends for harm done, turning our wills and lives over to God? Where did we learn about meditation and prayer and all the rest of it? The spiritual substance of our remaining ten Steps came straight from Dr. Bob's and my own earlier association with the Oxford Groups, as

they were then led in America by that Episcopal rector, Dr. Samuel Shoemaker.[3]

On April 23, 1963, Bill wrote a letter to Shoemaker, saying:

Certainly there were other indispensable contributions without which we should have probably got noplace. But none of these were so large or critical as your own. Though I wish the "co-founder" tag had never been hitched to any of us, I have no hesitancy in adding your name to the list! . . . The Twelve Steps of A.A. simply represented an attempt to state in more detail, breadth, and depth, what we had been taught, primarily by you. Without this, there could have been nothing–nothing at all.[4]

And A.A.'s Big Book says the following:

Though he could not accept all the tenets of the Oxford Groups, he [Bill Wilson] was convinced of the need for moral inventory, confession of personality defects, restitution to those harmed, helpfulness to others, and the necessity of belief in and dependence upon God.[5]

The Akron Link

What did Dr. Bob say about all this?

At his last major address to A.A. in Detroit in 1948, Dr. Bob stated:

We [Dr. Bob and Bill W.] had both been associated with the Oxford Group, Bill in New York, for five months, and I in Akron, for two and a half years. Bill had acquired their idea of service. I had not, but I had done an immense amount of reading they had recommended. I had refreshed my memory of the Good Book, and I had had excellent training in that as a youngster.[6]

I didn't write the Twelve Steps. I had nothing to do with the writing of them. But I think I probably had something to do with them indirectly. After my June 10th episode, Bill came to live at our house and stayed for about three months. There was hardly a night that we didn't sit up until two or three o'clock talking. . . . We already had the basic ideas, though not in terse and tangible form. We got them, as I said, as a result of our study of the Good Book.[7]

Anne Ripley Smith, Dr. Bob's wife, was often called the "mother of A.A." by Bill Wilson and by others.[8] Each morning, during the period Bill was living with the Smiths in the summer of 1935, Anne Smith "read and interpreted the Christian Scriptures and Oxford Group devotional books."[9] Both before and after the summer of 1935, Anne faithfully read, recorded, and wrote about Oxford Group and other Christian and Bible principles she was studying. She kept a "spiritual workbook," copies of which are located in A.A.'s archives in New York City and at Bill's home at Stepping Stones in Bedford Hills, New York. Recently discovered evidence makes it clear that Anne read the contents of her spiritual workbook to the alcoholics and their wives whom she and Dr. Bob helped in the Smith home.[10] In her workbook Anne specifically recommended the reading of four Shoemaker books—*Children of the Second Birth, Twice-Born Ministers, The Conversion of the Church,* and *If I Be Lifted Up.*[11] Sue Smith Windows, the Smiths' daughter, informed Dick B. that her father had read all the books his wife, Anne, recommended. And a copy of Shoemaker's book *Confident Faith,* which was owned and read by Dr. Bob, is still in the possession of the Smith family. In his last major address to A.A., Dr. Bob stated that he had done an immense amount of reading in books the Oxford Group had recommended.[12]

There is another Akron link to Shoemaker. Henrietta Seiberling, who was instrumental in getting Dr. Bob into the Oxford Group, was a frequent visitor at the Smith home.

She infused much spiritual education into Dr. Bob and Bill and led meetings they attended. Henrietta's son, former Congressman John F. Seiberling, informed Dick B., "My mother, I am sure, read all the Oxford Group books of the 1930s." And these included Shoemaker's books–many of which were specifically named by John Seiberling and his sisters, Mary and Dorothy.

The Calvary Evangel Link

The totality of what Bill W., Dr. Bob, Anne, and Henrietta Seiberling actually read and studied in the Bible, the Oxford Group, and the Shoemaker writings might be somewhat conjectural except for an Oxford Group literature list published in the Calvary Church's monthly parish publication. This journal was called *The Calvary Evangel*. It often listed Oxford Group literature and recommended it for reading. Mrs. Julia Harris, wife of Calvary Church's assistant minister, Rev. W. Irving Harris, was in charge of an Oxford Group "bookstore" located in the basement of Calvary House in New York, where most Oxford Group meetings were held. She informed Dick B. that the March 1939 Oxford Group literature list in *The Evangel* recorded all the Oxford Group books that were stocked at Calvary House and were sent out to those wishing Oxford Group literature. The *Evangel* list recommended the following Shoemaker books: *The Church Can Save the World, Children of the Second Birth, Twice-Born Ministers, If I Be Lifted Up, Confident Faith, The Gospel According to You, Religion That Works, The Conversion of the Church, National Awakening,* and *Realizing Religion.* There is every reason, from the remarks of Dr. Bob, of Dr. Bob's children, and of Henrietta Seiberling's children, to believe that Dr. Bob and Anne read all the foregoing Shoemaker books, and that Henrietta Seiberling did also.

What Sam Shoemaker Himself Had to Say

Of major historical significance is the fact that Sam Shoemaker wrote a letter to Bill Wilson on Calvary Rectory sta-
tionery, which is dated January 22, 1935. This date is less
than thirty days after Bill Wilson had his religious experience at Towns Hospital in December 1934, was relieved of
his obsession to drink, and began working with other alcoholics. We have eliminated last names from the Shoemaker
letter, which says:

> Dear Bill:
> I hope you realize the guidedness of your having known
> Jim W. previously, as I understand you did, in business.
> His wife, Margaret, is full time in the group and he has
> held out for a long while. You may be just the person that
> cracks the shell and brings him over. He drinks a lot and
> is desperately unhappy and inferior and needs what you
> have got for him. I am grateful for what you did for B.
> Yours ever,
Sam S.

At the very least, this letter indicates Shoemaker's early
knowledge of and support for Bill's work with alcoholics.
    On March 13, 1952, Dr. Shoemaker wrote a letter to
H. H. Brown, stating:

> Bill Wilson found his spiritual change in this House [Cal-
> vary House in New York] when the Oxford Group was
> at work here many years ago. I have had the closest touch
> with Bill from that day to this.[13]

On August 5, 1953, Shoemaker wrote Bill as follows:

> I never forgot that I was one of those who read the first
> mimeographed copy of the first book [*Alcoholics Anony-
> mous*]–I am afraid with considerable skepticism, for I

was then under the shadow of the old group feeling that unless a thing were done directly under the auspices of the group, it was as good as not done at all.[14]

Following his address at A.A.'s 20th anniversary convention in St. Louis, Shoemaker delivered a sermon entitled "What the Church Has to Learn from Alcoholics Anonymous." Among other things, he said:

It happens that I have watched the unfolding of this movement [the fellowship of AA] with more than usual interest, for its real founder and guiding spirit, Bill W., found his initial spiritual answer at Calvary Church in New York, when I was rector there, in 1935.

They say that each alcoholic holds within the orbit of his problem an average of fourteen persons who are affected by it. This means that conservatively two and a half million people's lives are different because of the existence of Alcoholics Anonymous.

AA indirectly derived much of its inspiration from the Church. Now perhaps the time has come for the Church to be re-awakened and revitalized by those insights and practices found in A.A.[15]

In his sermon Shoemaker said there are five things the church needs to learn from A.A.:

1. Nobody gets anywhere till he recognizes a clearly-defined need;
2. Men are redeemed in a life-changing fellowship;
3. There is the necessity for definite personal dealing with people;
4. There is the necessity for a real change of heart, a true conversion;

5. People have the need for an exposure to living Christian experience.[16]

Rev. Irving Harris's Memo of Wilson–Shoemaker Contacts

On April 7, 1992, Mrs. Irving Harris, widow of Sam Shoemaker's close associate, Rev. Irving Harris, wrote Dick B. and enclosed the following memorandum, which she said was an eyewitness account of her husband's observations of the relationship of Bill Wilson to Sam Shoemaker:

> While Bill never spent a single night at either Calvary House or at the Mission which Calvary Church maintained on East 23rd Street, New York, he owed much to the spiritual life generated at these places and even more to Sam Shoemaker, the man who headed up and fostered the activities at both centers.
>
> It was at a men's meeting at 61 Gramercy Park [Calvary House] that Bill's buddy, Ebbie Thatcher, felt the power of fellowship and experienced the inner assurance that he could "move out of the dark tunnel" of alcoholism; and it was at a meeting at Calvary Mission that Bill himself was moved to declare that he had decided to launch out as a follower of Jesus Christ.
>
> Then as he was establishing guidelines which he believed to be basic in maintaining sobriety, he frequently turned to Sam Shoemaker to talk over the relation between these early formulations of the Twelve Steps and the principles of the New Testament. Sam's friend, "Sherry" Day, had already outlined several principles of basic Christian living with which Bill was familiar.[17] As he discussed his counterparts to these he found that Sam's patient, quiet agreement put a seal on Bill's hope that these represented God's own truth. With a chuckle Sam would say something like, "Sounds like good old-fashioned Christian

faith, Bill." And Bill would perhaps reply, "Yes, it looks that way . . . almost too good to be true." These talks took place in Sam's book-lined seventh floor study at Calvary House with the door closed and the telephone switched off.

At that time in New York the usual result of a full-blown experience like Bill's consisted of full-time participation in the activities of one of the several Oxford Group traveling teams. And Bill's new friends in the Group frequently urged him to get going in the customary team activity.[18] Having shaken off the deadly grip of alcohol, he was consumed with a desire to spend his time not in general evangelism, or "life-changing," but in helping other alcoholics. He knew that many, many obsessive drinkers could find the same release and freedom which had come to him and it was to this work that he felt compelled to devote himself. And it was right here that Sam's counsel and backing proved so helpful. As one of the top American leaders of the old Group, Sam often had a deciding voice about where newly changed laymen might best tie in with the ever-extending work of the revival which was going on. He was impressed by the sincerity of Bill's own convictions about what he should do and advised him to follow his own deepest convictions even to the extent of incurring the disapproval of other leaders in the Group. In this Sam became Bill's special ally and "comforter," enabling him to withstand the pressures to conform. And by this, in God's providence, Sam shared in the steps which shortly led to the founding of Alcoholics Anonymous.[19]

How It Worked at Shoemaker's Calvary Church

At the present time there is not much eyewitness information as to how Wilson learned the Oxford Group principles from Rev. Sam Shoemaker at Calvary. That Bill Wilson learned them there seems abundantly clear from the statements of Bill, Shoemaker, and Harris. But how? Though Dr. Bob, Anne Smith, and Henrietta Seiberling apparently read all the Oxford Group books of the 1930s, including those of Sam Shoemaker, there are strong indications from the reminiscences of Bill's wife, Lois, and his secretary, Nell Wing, and from the dearth of Oxford Group literature present at Bill's Stepping Stones library that Bill himself read little if any Shoemaker literature.

So how were the Shoemaker teachings conveyed to Bill? Bill and his wife, Lois, attended Oxford Group meetings at Calvary House between late 1934 and 1937. And the meetings were sometimes led by Dr. Shoemaker and sometimes by his assistants, among whom were Rev. J. Herbert Smith and Rev. Irving Harris–both mentioned by Bill in letters and accounts. Bill was in the company of some leading Shoemaker lay friends or assistants, Hanford Twitchell, Rowland Hazard, F. Shepard Cornell, Philip Marshall Brown, Victor Kitchen, and Charles Clapp, Jr. These facts are only recently becoming evident from Lois Wilson's Oxford Group notes at Stepping Stones, from the writings of Irving Harris, from the recollections of Jim Newton, and even perhaps from indications in Victor Kitchen's book, *I Was a Pagan.*

But we turn now to F. Shepard Cornell, a former alcoholic, who was a member of the Oxford Group business team in New York; was a vestryman in Shoemaker's church; was frequently listed as a sponsor on Oxford Group house party programs and invitations; was listed in Bill's address book at Stepping Stones; was a frequent attender of Oxford Group meetings with Bill, his wife, Lois, and Ebby Thatcher; and was with Bill and Ebby just before Bill got sober. What did "Shep" Cornell share with Bill? Bill never said. But another alcoholic who was present at Calvary about the time Bill was recovering did talk about working with Shep Cornell. This man was Charles Clapp, Jr. In his book, *The Big Bender,* Clapp tells of working with Cornell, sharing that experience with Rev. Sam Shoemaker, and also about meeting another recovered alcoholic. The latter may have been Bill Wilson since Wilson was the Oxford Group person in those days who was giving special emphasis to personal work with alcoholics.

We have included a chapter containing part of Clapp's story for what light it may shed on how the Oxford Group message was being carried at Sam Shoemaker's Calvary Church, Calvary House, and Calvary Rescue Mission.

For the reader's benefit, we have excerpted portions of Bill Wilson's story as he wrote it in the first edition of A.A.'s Big Book, published in 1939. There are interesting similarities between Bill's story and that of Charles Clapp, Jr.—both of whom were very much in touch with Calvary in the 1934–1935 period. We have no way of knowing at this stage of historical research whether Bill, like Clapp, actually shared with Shoemaker or whether Bill simply heard Shoemaker at meetings as Clapp did, and then enhanced his knowledge of Oxford Group principles and Shoemaker teachings by listening to and sharing with Shoemaker's assistants, "Jack" Smith and Irving Harris, and Shoemaker's church leaders, such as Hanford Twitchell, Rowland Hazard, and Shep Cornell.

In any event, our book will let Sam Shoemaker share in his own words the kinds of things he was teaching that seem to have become embodied in A.A.'s Twelve Steps and with which he was credited by Bill Wilson.

The Approach of This Book

Many benefits can come from an examination of Shoemaker's own words, which exhorted others to have the courage to change.

First, the reader can see Shoemaker's own approach to a conversion experience, expressed in words that must have captured the thinking and action of A.A.'s co-founders.

Second, A.A. members who read Shoemaker's words will very probably see familiar language, similar to that in their own Big Book and in the writings of Bill Wilson.

Third, Shoemaker's beautiful way of expressing the move from estrangement from God to a new and vital experience of God should give new hope to the seemingly hopeless.

Fourth, Shoemaker's words should give new insight on the spiritual principles and spiritual experience A.A.'s found necessary for their recovery from alcoholism.

Fifth, for those in the clergy who would like an insight as to how a man of the cloth was able to bring the message of Christian deliverance to so many in the deathly throes of alcoholism, Shoemaker's own approach could be of assistance.

Sixth, recovery centers, doctors, therapists, correctional workers, and family counselors should benefit from knowing more of the spiritual principles Shoemaker espoused.

Seventh, Shoemaker's *What the Church Has to Learn from Alcoholics Anonymous* should be of help to all denominations.

Finally, we hope this work will challenge others to delve still more into the rich spiritual history of A.A.

Note that in many of the excerpts contained in his book, Shoemaker tells the stories of anonymous recovering alcoholics. The pronouns "he" and "I" used in these stories refer to those people.

1

Estrangement from God

Step One: We admitted we were powerless over alcohol–that our lives had become unmanageable.

There is a way that seemeth right unto a man, but the end thereof are the ways of death.

Proverbs 16:25

Thou madest us for Thyself, and our heart is restless, until it repose in Thee.

St. Augustine

Sam Shoemaker appears to have written little about the disease of alcoholism. But his life records much compassion for alcoholics and deep interest in helping them recover by spiritual means. In 1926 he established Calvary Mission in the "Gas House District" where, as it was said, "There is a place nearby where a Carpenter still mends broken men." There Bill Wilson's "sponsor," Ebby Thatcher, and Bill Wilson himself, first surrendered their lives to God in the plain hall dominated by a great wooden cross on the front wall. There, night after night, men once despondent gave messages of salvation through Jesus Christ.

Sam Shoemaker personally led Russell Firestone, an alcoholic, to a decision for Christ on a train ride from Denver to Akron. The event led, in 1933, to the arrival of an Oxford Group team in Akron. This visit was accompanied by widespread publicity about Firestone's life-change through application of the Oxford Group's Christian principles and practices. We quote at length in this book from Charles Clapp Jr.'s *The Big Bender,* in which Clapp recounts his personal work with Sam Shoemaker and Clapp's victory over alcoholism. We've already noted Shoemaker's early personal interest in Bill Wilson's efforts to help alcoholics—efforts that began almost the moment Wilson was released from Towns Hospital in 1934, having whipped alcoholism via the very kind of vital religious experience Shoemaker had previously espoused to Wilson's friends.

What did Shoemaker contribute to First Step thinking? The answer may lie in his books about man's defeat, despair, and spiritual misery. These occur when self-reliance fails and man is restless and discontented, estranged from God, and hamstrung by an unmanageable life—a condition for which alcohol offers a deadly solution to the alcoholic. Shoemaker once helped an "east-sider" named Charlie, a young Italian. No one knows for sure what Shoemaker said to Charlie; but new life came when Charlie made a simple plea: "God manage me, 'cause I can't manage myself." Charlie's prayer contained First Step elements of which Shoemaker often wrote: the need for honesty, childlike humility, and a cry for help in order to receive the vital religious experience that can bring man to God.

A very short time after his own conversion, he was asked to go and see a man in Boston who was suffering from the after-agonies of drink at the time. This man came of people of great refinement and wealth, he had begun to drink during the war, he had married and lost his wife, and drink was the only way he knew in which he could drown the sense of futility and emptiness of his life. Medicine and psychiatry had helped, but they seemed unable to get at the root-motives which would give the man the desire to change, coupled with hope about himself. He was in the care of a male nurse, when "From the Far Country" first saw him. He talked with him a little at a time, as he was able and ready to listen to a story, the forepart of which was so much like his own. He was persuaded to come to a house-party which was being held at Narragansett Pier. There he met the Militant Mystic and several other men who were trying to live the Christian life. He liked them. One day when almost crying for another drink, "From the Far Country," who had been the custodian of his bottle and given him a drink when it was medically necessary (think of this man, himself a drunkard less than a month before!) said to him lovingly and firmly, "No, old man. We are through with that now. We are going to get down on our knees and ask God to take away the craving." Three of them knelt down. The third man prayed aloud, very simply, very sincerely. It shook the man they wanted to reach, to the bottom of his soul. He made his decision for Christ. Today he is a victorious spirit, giving his life to winning men, and is on a mission to university students in South Africa as this book goes to the publisher (TBM, 169–70).

A few nights ago I sat with a man who has been living a Christian life for years, but who has never yet got a clean victory from sin and the fear of sin. So representative is his situation, with his heart right and fundamentally wanting to live as a Christian, and yet downed again and again by his gusts of temptation and moodiness, that he may well stand for many of us here this morning. I have talked with

him many and many a time, and I have always before urged
upon him that the way out lay through a profounder surrender of himself. Surrender is merely faith active: it is the
act by which the desire of faith turns into determination,
and it has to be made before the forces of grace can oper-
ate in any human life. But the oft-repeated surrender of self
to God, without a corresponding increase in understanding how much God has already done for our redemption,
is only flogging the human will to greater activity. This time
I said nothing to him of further surrender. I said that we
had been putting our final trust in our own faith, and not
in God's grace: and we had got second things first. I urged
upon him this time a full recognition that God's redemption was available to him whensoever he chose to appropriate it, and I asked him to commit himself this time to
nothing, but only to accept in faith the great fact of salvation from God. I told him that I knew that if he would make
that act in faith, he would find himself not the possessor of,
but possessed by, a Force outside himself, greater than himself, independent of his moods and his sudden seizures of
temptation. Again and again he came back, "But what if I
fail again?" And each time I said, "But when you come to
the Cross this way, you claim the power of Christ's redemption and His Holy Spirit. The connection has been made:
you are no longer your own, you have no further responsibility than to make and preserve the connection. The crux
of your spiritual problem from now on lies in daily, hourly
re-appropriation of the power of the Cross." And then I said,
"Will you kneel here with me, and claim as yours the full
power of Christ's Cross, and trust Him to keep you, as you
have not been able to keep yourself?" He said that he would,
and he took that step.

Someone will say to me, "Ah, yes, but the test will come
later." That is very true. It is one thing to ride for a few days
or weeks in the splendid carriage of a new spiritual conviction, and quite another to stay in it and be borne along

in it all our lives. I know no sinless Christians, though I know a few who fancy themselves to be such. "If we say that we have no sin, we deceive ourselves, and the truth is not in us." Yet we must complete the verse, "But if we confess our sins, God is faithful and just to forgive us our sins, and to cleanse us from *all unrighteousness.*" The life of true victory in Christ must ever be the prayed-for and expected aim of every Christian's life. There is such a thing as a spiritual rebirth which carries with it an assurance of God's power to master sin for us, and which belongs in the realm of sheer spiritual miracle. So long as our last authority in religion is the word or encouragement of some other life, or the testimony of our fluctuating emotions, we shall have our moral slippings and slidings, our theological ins and outs, our spiritual ups and downs. But if we find the Cross as the "power of God unto salvation," and plant our faith there, and there claim the releasing power of the Holy Spirit, we move up into another region than the poor realm of our will-power, even when it is buttressed by prayer and the helps of ordinary religious faith. The life that finds this assurance is twice-blest: once, in the joy and peace of the deliverance itself and then in the knowledge that it has come "*by* grace *through* faith—not of ourselves—it is the gift of God" (IIBL, 175–78).

For who are the blind? Which is worse, not to see faces and hills and sunsets or not to see that *you* are the chief source of your own difficulty in life: if you were different, life would be; not to see that human nature itself can and must be changed; not to see the hand of God moving in history and in one's own life; not to see what is the real problem, and the way to solve it, when our friends are in need? *That* is blindness. . . . Begin looking inward and upward, instead of outward and downward, and you will find the real question and the real answer. How many blind people have I sat with, and put the simplest of truth before them, and watched a new dawn break over their lives, and heard them say simply and with understanding, "I see!" (NA, 30).

Not long since I saw a young man dissipating his life away in drink. I saw him later exposed to a group of people who made ideals attractive to him, so that he deeply wanted to live by those ideals, and declared vehemently that he intended to do so. I warned him that I had seen too many men try to resolve themselves out of sin, and inevitably fall back into it. I saw a new look come into his face, a look of guilt, and then of dependence on God. I saw him give up all notions that he could possibly live up to the ideals he admired, and hand his life to God. And I have had the joy of seeing him find a growing victory and peace in our Lord Jesus Christ (CF, 162).

2

Came to Believe

Step Two: Came to believe that a Power greater than ourselves could restore us to sanity.

But without faith it is impossible to please him: for he that cometh to God must believe that he is, and that he is a rewarder of them that diligently seek him.

Hebrews 11:6

If any man will do his will, he shall know of the doctrine, whether it be of God, or whether I speak of myself.

John 7:17

Shoemaker approached faith by teaching that it involves an experiment. He said that to come to and to know God, man has to believe that God is. Man can come to believe by being willing to believe. But the willingness has to be

31

evidenced by action—seeking God by obedience to His known will. Man is to listen. God will speak. Man is to obey, and God will act. Man can validate his assumption as to God's existence and power, can move from belief to knowing, through experiencing God's power and presence as the result of conducting the experiment of faith.

Faith in a personal and loving God, is the one thing which steps up to the vague longing of the human heart for solace, for people, for joy, and says, "I am what you are looking for. 'I am He Whom thou seekest.' You are homesick for God" (GATY, 108).

Well, then, how shall we come to have a faith like that?

We need to remember first, I think, that faith is not primarily an intellectual but a moral matter. It is much more like loyalty than it is like philosophy. Its basis is not thought, nor correlated thought, but experience based on experiment. People who read great books about God do not always find God, and they fail because they want to find ready-made a coherent system of thought about life. Faith does not begin that way. Philosophy may begin that way, but religion begins as life does, with a cry of hunger—and reason comes long after. The real enemy of faith is not reason, but inexperience; it is not an overgrown mentality, it is an underdone experience. All intellectual formulations of religion come long after the initial experience of religion. You must begin with the experience. You must begin with searching your own heart for what stands in the place of God, for the things that would drive faith away if it approached, which could not stay in the same life and keep company with it. You will be surprised the way your rational difficulties begin to clear up if you get your moral difficulties straightened out first. When first some of you at the university went into a chemical laboratory, you did what the professor told you to do, and the predictions he made came true: you judged of materials, not by what they were (of that you knew as yet nothing) but by what they did. It is so in religion. Listen to the spiritually experienced, who have themselves tried the experiment, and you will find that it turns out for you in the same way (GATY, 126–27).

When a person tells me they don't believe, I say, What kind of a life are you living? If the sun seems dim to you, it may be the windows are dirty. You cannot shorten the 93,000,000 miles, but you can wash the windows. God may be dim to you because your own windows need washing (GATY, 165–66).

Let my friend, whom I shall quote frequently in this book, speak of the intimate heart-hungers which self-made religion did not satisfy. "I want freedom to live sanely and beautifully and serenely and well. . . . I thought I had found stability after my first period of doubt a few years ago, in my personal code of ethics, my half-agnostic philosophy. But that house was not founded on a rock. My principles 'listened' well but they worked like the devil's own. It was in talking to you that I realized the horror I was passing through, and suddenly gave up that path because I saw it ending in a blank wall or worse." One is reminded of a very old verse: "There is a way which seemeth right unto a man, but the end thereof are the ways of death." And complete honesty would bring forth from many as frank a confession of their failure to find any help in a religion which they are seeking to work out alone.

Every aspiring soul wants "freedom to live sanely and beautifully and serenely and well." All the fussiness and clambering of life, physical and mental uneasiness, discontent, triviality, jarring of wills within the home, that elusive and permeating unrest of our day—we know it is all wrong. Something is lacking. Somehow we have missed the way.

Yes, life is complex—but we know that if our souls were sim-
pler our lives would be better ordered. We buy and spend
and travel to get away from ourselves. The trouble is within,
not without. We may be dissatisfied with our surroundings,
or our failures, or our handicaps. But most of all, we are
"dissatisfied with ourselves."

It is clear to see what people like my friend want. They
want to have life swung from the far Center. They want an
anchor, a guide, a foundation. Confessing defeat, they long
for a leader surer than themselves, who has trod this way
before them, and trod it well. They want a great passion and
a great love, something to harmonize and reconcile life,
something to put good will and optimism and power into
it, something to quiet their tempers and order their homes
and fill them with hope and calm.

It is like telling Naaman to go and wash seven times in
the Jordan to tell them that what they want is perfectly well
known, perfectly accessible. All of us cling, despite all proofs
to the contrary, to the idea that we are different, and need
something that others do not need, and never can be satisfied with any generally accepted ideas about religion. But
this is our old pride raising its head for a last thrust. Our
heavenly Father knows where we are really different.

What you want is simply a vital religious experience. You
need to find God (RR, 7–9).

Almost all men are slaves: they are mastered by foolish
ambitions, vile appetites, jealousies, prejudices, the conventions and opinions of other men. These things obsess
them, so that they cannot see anything in its true perspective. For most men the world is centered in self, which is
misery: to have the world centered in God is the peace that
passeth understanding. This is liberty: to know that God
alone matters (RR, 11).

Faith is the permanent attitude of mind towards God of a person who has surrendered to Him; it is not so much an intellectual quality as it is a resolute fixture of the will to listen to Him and to obey Him. The fiery darts of the wicked are the darts of sin, of doubt, of discouragement, of self-will, of temptation to run your own life, of envying others, of disloyalty to God; and he sends them at all of us as often as possible, because our failure in these means our going over to antichrist. But against the shield of faith, of surrender to God, the darts fall lifeless (GC, 31).

The way out of unbelief is moral as well as intellectual. Jesus said, "If any man willeth to do his will, he shall know." That is to say, "If any man will begin by living up to as much as he understands of the moral requisites of God, he will later, in the light of his experience, come to see straight intellectually." That is an experimental challenge, and it has been the experience of thousands upon thousands that it is an experiment which leads to truth for life. I may be quite unable to convince a man he is wrong in not believing in God or in the divinity of Christ: if I can get him to live according to the revealed will of the God in whom as yet he cannot believe, time will come when he will believe in that God and understand with his mind. A moral experiment is worth ten times an intellectual investigation in apprehending spiritual truth. Obedience is as much the organ of spiritual understanding as reason. Many people have come into a personal and living faith by trying the experiment which is implied in: "If any man willeth to do his will, he shall know."

Unbelief, therefore, is not naked intellectual doubt: it is compounded with moral refusal to proceed upon the evidence of the experience of others. It is as much a matter of temperament, oftentimes, as of reason. And it often has its seat more in the will than in the mind. Unbelief is the negative atmosphere, the unexpectant, unhopeful attitude (RTW, 36–37).

Unbelief isn't doubting some fact of long ago—unbelief is acting and feeling as though there were no God in the daily conduct of our lives. You can believe in miracles in the New Testament and the Old; but if you cannot believe in miracles in your own life, your faith is cold. . . . Against the evidence of facts rises up this mood, this misgiving, this fear out of some dark place in my own heart. And that doubt for me is sin—sin against which I have to fight as against any other sin. . . . When I doubt it, the fear arises, not from outside myself where I cannot control it, but from inside myself where I can (RTW, 38–39).

Let us come to grips with the unbelief in our own lives—not the questioning of this or that miracle or point of theology—those may need to wait till larger matters are settled. I mean unbelief about God and life and the goodness of the universe and the worthwhileness of life. If you question here, ask yourself very honestly how much sin enters into your doubt—sin of intellectual pride, sin of self-pity which loves to think itself injured in an unjust cosmos, sin of laziness which will not really investigate, sin of fear which will not face God lest He ask of us that which we are unwilling to grant. I do not say this to condemn you, but to reveal you to yourselves. Be quite honest whether this seems to you a wholly reasonable way to look at religion. . . . Is that what you are doing? Have you sought out people He has helped, and found out how it came? Or have you gone off skulking and said religion was all humbug and emotion (RTW, 40–41)?

I should like to live always in the high place of *faith*. I do not mean the low hills of assent to inherited theological propositions, but the high hill of such trust in God as literally transfigures the earth. I mean the faith which refuses ever to consider any situation a trap, but views each one as a crucible in which some creative event may take place . . .

which sees advantages wrapped in limitations, and man's extremity as God's opportunity which He will not fail to improve.

I mean the faith which sees through the outwardness of sorrow to its inwardness, and finds a meaning for the deepest loss. . . . I mean the faith that cannot be shaken of its inward harmony and tranquility by any outward misfortune or neglect or hostility: but that has a foundation in another world, utterly independent of what man can do unto it.

I mean the faith which is sure of the final conquest of good over evil—sure of it because the quantity of evil is outweighed by the quality of good, and because God is God (RTW, 121).

He asks us to begin with Him at the known and follow Him into the unknown . . . There would be no such thing as real faith if faith were sight, if it were certainty of happiness, if it were insurance against trouble. . . . Begin where you can (IIBL, 22).

The faith that holds through the dark hour is a much stronger faith, a much riper and maturer faith, one much better gauged for the whole of our life. It depends upon where and what we are, how Christ comes to us. Sometimes we are enough like children to have faith come in upon a wave of joy, and we remember to be thankful. Sometimes we are hard and self-sufficient, and nothing but sorrow will ever reduce our pride and self-reliance, and make us know how helpless we really are without God. . . . Either way, do believe that God is knocking for an entrance into your life. If you can grasp it by joy, then take it: but if you cannot, then look for it in your trouble; it will be only a blessing in disguise if God can use it as His indirect way of touching you, and causing you to seek Him just because you are so miserable without Him (IIBL, 23–24).

Faith in God and in man will stand us in better stead than
to look within and lean upon the uncertain staff of our own
pride (IIBL, 35).

Then we may have gone yet a step farther, and seen that
faith is a kind of leap out toward God, in which the will also
is involved: so that faith has become for us the function of
the whole man, mind and heart and will: it is an attitude
toward life and the Unseen in which all our powers are
implicated. So strong is this faculty in full health, so filled
with the power to recreate the life in which it is found res-
ident, that it sometimes takes the central place in the Christian's life. We have many a time seen faith fairly create the
things in which it believes: that is why it is called in Hebrews
"the substance of things hoped for, the evidence of things
not seen" (IIBL, 173).

And where is it [our security]? It lies in a faith in God
which includes an experiment. It lies in believing that God
is, that He has a plan, and that He will reveal that plan to
us. It lies in fitting in with that plan ourselves, and finding
that God will take care of us when we dare to make that
experiment. . . . Many people believe in God as a kind of
background to the universe: but that remains only a lifeless
concept until you move forward on the logic of it to believe
in a God still creating, still creating partly by redeeming—a
God with a definite plan in His mind for every life, every
decision, every problem, that can arise on earth—a plan for
the settlement of peace between nations in conflict, for the
avoidance of war in Europe, for settling a strike in New
York. Nobody ever got much out of believing in a God Who
just looks on. Real faith begins when we trust a God Who
works into modern life through individuals. The kind of
security we are talking about depends upon our own action
in concert with such a God. You will never find it in sitting
still. You will never find it by believing in a God Who sits

still. A God with a plan—with definite, accurate, adequate information for people who want to see that plan fulfilled—that is the groundwork of true security (NA, 40–41).

I say that what does not work is not true. I am driven reasonably towards faith by the utter practical failures of unbelief. . . . But it is life which is causing our difficulty, not religion. Life is asking the questions, religion is offering the answer. . . . Who *are* we? What *are* we doing here? Where *do* we belong? Religion did not ask those questions. Life asked them, and goes on asking them. Religion offers an answer. Some of you hold off from religious faith because you cannot find a definition of God, or because you can't believe in miracles, or think the Christian theology too complex to swallow, or because you find some hypocrites in the Christian church. These are very small fry in comparison with what answer you shall return to those basic questions life asks. Are you willing to make answer, "I am a biological accident, a hundred and fifty pounds of chemicals; I am not doing anything, but am the sport of uncontrollable physical forces; and I was born, live and die a tiny fragment of blind brute creation"? Or will you answer, "I am a child of God, and I am here working out my own salvation and that of others, and I belong to the great family of believers, here and beyond" (CF, 101–102)?

And if I am wise, I remember what science tells me, that all knowledge comes by hypothesis and experiment: and I try the experiment. And I discover that the further I go with it, the surer I am that it is the truth. I begin my turn towards Christ in a kind of despair of everything else, like Simon Peter when he said, "Lord, to whom shall we go? Thou hast the words of eternal life." But as time goes on, faith grows, till I can say with the Samaritans of old, "I know that this is indeed the Christ, the Saviour of the world."

And when I have done this, I have not given my mind an anaesthetic: I have used it. I have made it work, not only upon theoretical problems, but upon the realistic problems of actual life. Jesus was in earnest when He said, "Thou shalt love the Lord thy God . . . with all thy mind." Yes, with *all* of it, pure reason and practical reason: cold logic and warm imagination. The opposite of reason is not always emotion: sometimes it is imagination, and of this all reasonable people make use. But the place where all reason comes to an end is the place where the experiment begins: Bernard Shaw is right: action goes beyond reason, and verifies it. The faculty of faith is required when you step from hypothesis to experiment. You can't tell whether the ice will hold you till you step out on it. But faith is supplanted by knowledge when the experiment works. It is so in science, and it is so in life.

I have had no time to deal with the moral factor in unbelief. A great many people are wondering today how their minds can begin to have faith in God, and they want logical proof. One wants to say to them that their lives are too self-centered, too dirty, too dishonest, too hard, to believe in God. The pure in heart see God. He that willeth to do His will shall know of the doctrine. Anyone who loves anything else better than God cannot believe in God. Anyone who does not know God, and insists upon carrying over into faith some habit or attitude which comes before God for him, will never know God. Your difficulty may lie, not in your mind, but in your life.

God help us all to believe in Him with all our heart and all our soul and all our mind—to know that there is no divorce between one kind of truth and another—to use our minds, all of our minds, upon all of the facts—and to pray as we think—so that we may know the truth, and the truth may make us free (CF, 105–106).

3

The Decision
to Surrender

Step Three: Made a decision to turn our will and our lives over to the care of God *as we understood Him.*

Be still, and know that I am God; I will be exalted among the heathen, I will be exalted in the earth.
Psalm 46:10

"Give in," he cries, "admit that I am God, high over nations, high over the world."
Psalm 46:10 (Moffatt)

Thy will be done.
Matthew 6:10

Shoemaker believed that seeking and surrendering to God starts with a decision. One does not need fully to understand God. He can surrender as much of himself as he can to as much of God as he understands. Then, said Shoemaker, his decision must be to "give in," to abandon himself to God, to let go. He must take the position that God is God and self is not. Shoemaker suggested that the decision can be embodied in the language of the Lord's Prayer: Thy will be done.

Finally, on the evening of August 23, I attended a Thursday night group meeting, and it was there that I heard two clergymen speak, one of whom was a bishop. What these two men said rendered the knock-out blow to my pride, and after the meeting I walked home with the rector, determined to make a surrender of my life. This conversion business puzzled me. I did not know how to go about it, and I was too timid to ask. I could not conceive of anything happening to me such as happened to St. Paul in apostolic times. But in our conversation we got down to "brass tacks," and before long I had brought out into the open a number of what we old-fashionedly call *sins,* which were blocking me from communion with God. Right then and there I surrendered those specific sins and all the others which I might discover later but which I could not recall or recognize then as sins. Both of us got down on our knees, he praying for me first, and then I prayed for God's forgiveness and without any reservations I handed my life over to God for Him to use as He saw fit—not as I saw fit. There was no white light, and not a great deal of emotion, but immediately there came a feeling of peace and release. But I know all too well that I cannot ride on the glory of that first surrender for the remainder of my life. It is not a question of being converted once and for all time, but rather it is a question of successively giving up new areas as the realization comes that you have been "holding out on God." It is by this means that Guidance becomes more and more real and that one feels more and more the Power of God's Holy Spirit taking possession (TBM, 29–30).

This experience, which I consider was my conversion, brought to me a kind of life which was entirely new to me. The fears were proved foolish. There was an integration of scattered impulses. I had victory where I never expected to have it. The daily Quiet Times helped tremendously in concentration and the ordering of each day. I was given the power, through sharing to the limit of my own experience, of helping others in a way which had been impossible on the old basis of human companionship only. Theology became vital, and preparation for the ministry a romance of discovery and expectation. The Church and the Bible had a new meaning. Such sayings as, "Ye must be born again," and "He that loseth his life for my sake ... shall find it," and "Seek ye first the kingdom ... and all these things shall be added," became living to me as part of my own experience. Previously I had gone just far enough into Christianity to feel the burden of the law, and not far enough to reap the joy of the Spirit. Now things were different (TBM, 55–56).

I wish that I had known then what I know now, that God shows His will only *decision by decision*, day by day. One only gets the full picture as he strikes out on what he has and knows. God never lets us down—it's safe to trust those inner urgings,—safer than we know (TBM, 112).

For the first time the conflict was resolved, the rift in his conscience was healed, the two sides of his life came together; and he was at one with himself when he gave himself to the doing of God's will (TBM, 121).

I knew that I needed to face a complete and unreserved surrender in my own life, and I did it after being perfectly

honest with that man about my own inner life as I knew
God saw me.

Conversion may be the work of a moment, but the implications of it are the work of a lifetime. The Fellowship real-
izes this truth, and helps in every way to see that surrender
only begins a long warfare. There is need for daily surrender (TBM, 149).

Decision . . . means, of course, giving all their sins and
problems to God, taking a different "way" the rest of their
lives, and trusting God for all that they cannot see at the
time. Our own faith that such an act may mean a turning-
point for this life will be contagious: one sign of misgiving,
or too much preoccupation on our part with the next stages
of the struggle, will be enough to prevent a great decision
from being made (TBM, 187–88).

The heart of surrender does not lie in asking God to take
our problems and solve them for us because we have been
unable to do so: it lies in giving ourselves to Him for the
doing of His will. If you surrender to find peace, you probably will not find it (GATY, 86).

And finally remember always that the true meaning of
faith is self-surrender to God. It is not a view-point, it is a
commitment. Dean Inge says, "Faith is an act of self-consecration, in which the will, the intellect, and the affections
all have their place." An act of self-consecration—not a
notion of spiritual curiosity, not a fixity of rational outlook—
an act of self-consecration. Surrender to whatever you know
about Him, or believe must be the truth about Him. Surrender to Him, if necessary, in total ignorance of Him. Far
more important that you touch Him than that you understand Him at first. Put yourself in His hands. Whatever He
is, as William James said, He is more ideal than we are.
Make the leap. Give yourself to Him. Remember how much

of stubborn pride underlay your unbelief; after they are changed so many people tell me of the flimsy, unlovely arguments with which their pride used to bolster up their unbelief, and how the deepest element in their surrender was the murder of that pride. The real reason why thousands of people do not and say they "cannot" believe is that they do not want God with all their hearts, but something else stands in their way. If St. Paul that day outside Damascus' walls had bargained with His Lord, and told the Risen Christ to wait upon some plan Paul had in his mind, he should never have come where he could write the words we are thinking about to-day. When he saw Christ, he gave in—all of him, and for all time. God gave back to him in full measure of faith all that Saul gave of himself to God. Religion is like love in that respect—it increases by self-giving. No wonder Christ defined it in the terms of love, not of abstract truth; of relationship, not of reason. You can only discover a relationship as you progressively give yourself to that person. And that is true with God, also.

Let us never forget that God is more anxious to find us—the least of us, the most wayward of us—than we are to find Him. Without tampering with our freedom, He is always seeking a way into our hearts. He wants to come with all His power and all His gladness. He wants to give us His gift of faith, so that amid the perplexities and difficulties and sorrows of this time, and of all time, we can be calm and triumphant within, and be ourselves "persuaded that neither death, nor life, nor angels, nor principalities, nor powers, nor things present, nor things to come, nor height, nor depth, nor any other creature, shall be able to separate us from the love of God which is in Christ Jesus our Lord."

God grant us that faith in abundant measure (GATY, 128–30)!

"Ye must be born again." That imperative is a judgment against those who withstand conversion. But it is a hope held out to those fearful and self-depreciating people who do not think themselves capable of conversion. The new life begins by utter self-dedication to the will of God. All of us can do that, and must (RTW, 14).

We do not know Him, nor have we really found Him. And I believe the trouble lies here: we have not surrendered ourselves to Him. There is something within us He hates, and we will not let it go. There is a plan He has for us bigger than our own plan, and we are afraid of it. Somewhere we hold back. Somewhere we keep control of our own destiny. Let go! Abandon yourself to Him. Say to Him, "Not my will but Thine be done." Live it. Pray for it (RTW, 19).

We know that when we surrender with our whole wills, something happens that never wholly disappears. New ground is taken which we never entirely lose.

But we know, too, that such a decision of the will does not insure that we shall always be able to keep our emotions in line with it (IIBL, 94).

A man is born again when the control of his life, its center and its direction pass from himself to God (NA, 57).

I found out that conversion was not a remote and isolated incident in the life of St. Paul, but a very widespread and common experience. I learned that these experiences varied immensely in their details, but were often surprisingly alike in their essentials. I began to look for the universal essentials. I found that in its main outlines St. Paul's conversion conformed to many others: namely in the need which preceded it, the divided life, sharpening into a sense of sin and the need for forgiveness. And in the willing surrender of the self to God and His mercy and His plan, as represented in the words, "What shall I do, Lord?" And in the action of God upon that open soul, the change God makes, the forgiveness He gives, the peace that follows. And in all the subsequent life, of inward unity and deep joy, of outward righteousness and service, of steady witnessing to the Power which has saved and kept, and of perpetual contact with Christ. These things are not the special accidents of the conversion of one man, they are the essential factors in the conversion of all men. For they are open to all men. And happy is the man who travels the road which winds its way through them (CF, 115–16)!

4

Self-Examination and Confession

Step Four: Made a searching and fearless moral inventory of ourselves.

And why beholdest thou the mote that is in thy brother's eye, but considerest not the beam that is in thine own eye? ... Thou hypocrite, first cast out the beam out of thine own eye; and then shalt thou see clearly to cast out the mote out of thy brother's eye.

Matthew 7:3, 5

Step Five: Admitted to God, to ourselves, and to another human being the exact nature of our wrongs.

Confess your faults one to another.

James 5:16

Sin, said Shoemaker, is that which blocks a person from
God and from others. And the path back to a relationship
with God must be freed of the blocks or barriers. He said
most people are up against some clearly defined sins—
grudges, fears, selfishness, dishonesty. Shoemaker advocated taking a piece of paper and measuring one's life
against the Oxford Group's Four Absolutes—honesty,
purity, unselfishness, and love—to identify where one has
fallen short and blocked out God. Upon completion of the
list, one must be honest about those sins with God and with
another human being. These two steps—self-examination
and the honest sharing of sins with another—are necessary to put one on the path away from self-centeredness
to God-centeredness.

He gave me the four absolute principles of Christ: honesty, purity, unselfishness and love, and asked me how my
life stacked up beside them. I saw that here was a man who
could help me out of my troubles, and I told him all about
myself. Next he said:

"Have you ever surrendered yourself to Christ?" I had
not, but I decided that now was the time to do so. The result
was such an experience as I had never had before. . . .

It was very definitely a turning-point in my life. For the
first time here was someone who was willing to sit down
and talk with me alone, who somehow knew how to get
down to the levels I needed to talk on. I told him many of
the things I was ashamed of, which were troubling me,
revealing to him my ignorance of the world and of myself.
I told him all but one thing. "Is that all there is to talk
about?" he said. I declared it was. Then in a moment, and
in a very friendly way, he said, "Tom, you lied just now,
didn't you?" How glad I was that he asked, so that I might
admit that he was right, and then tell him the whole business. The release and happiness that came to me that night
had been unknown before. Later, at a house-party, came

another surrender of a boyhood dream of becoming famous: it was not entirely bad, but it was unrelated to my present life, and it was bad *for me.* I shared there also with another fellow in college, and I saw the futility of being educated but with a rotten core inside. . . . [He] has given of his entire self to me–his house, his food, money, time, thought, care and, best of all, his spiritual vision of what I can become (TBM, 150–51).

I never learned more about religious work than I learned from Frank Buchman when he said, "the first and fundamental need is ourselves." It is so much easier to skip this first requirement, and go on to ask what comes next. The whole process has got to begin with us. For a good many it must begin with a fresh sense of sin, and we might safely question ourselves about professional ambition, discouragement and self-pity, grudges against authorities or members of our congregation, our dispositions at home, physical and intellectual laziness, intemperance, sins of the flesh and of the mind, compromise in preaching, want of private prayer and Bible study, favouritism, and a spirit of harsh judgment. We shall never do effectual work with other people except as it begins in an experience of our own: and we may need to seek out that honest soul whom we trust more than any one else to say the truth to us, and in the way appropriate to us, make a clean breast of the facts about ourselves, a "confession," if you call it that, but let there be no spirit of "Haven't I confessed enough?" for that will defeat the whole purpose: let it come out, all of it, without justification or excuse–begin with yourself at rock bottom, and no pride left.

Then we shall need to make a new surrender which involves the break with our particular sins, and includes restoration and restitution, confession and forgiveness, where they are necessary. Those times of self-humiliation are the most unlovely and unwelcome hours of the Chris-

tian life; but they grow power and joy and peace, as rotten
earth grows roses (TBM, 182–83).

I ask you to do this. Hold yourself at arm's length—you,
whether you have been to church all your life or whether
you never go. Take a good look at your outer self and then
make an impartial report to your inner self of just what you
saw. Tell yourself frankly just how much plain, black, unmistakable sin you found, and how much that has had to do
with the restlessness and fretting and trifling disquietude in
yourself, in the circle that swings about you—that is, the circle of your influence, and especially your home. Stand this
off against complaint about other people's dispositions and
circumstances, and your bank balance, and ask yourself
how much you are the cause of this misery within and without. Of course we are better than many others similarly
placed. That is the Pharisee's test. He found nothing amiss.
Do we (RR, 18)?

It was the consciousness of personal sin which drew from
my friend these pathetic and tremendously healthy words:
"Oh! to be made over in the Spirit! I want a rebirth, but it
comes not in one agony. Oh! how I want freedom from these
deadening doubts, from this horrible, haunting sense, no,
knowledge of sin—this hopeless self-hatred and suffering!
. . . My eyes are so beclouded with conscious sin that I cannot see the light. I hope the redemption will come."
    And Dr. McComb, whose skill at helping people in spir-
itual need makes him one of the marked religious forces of
our day, has said: "At the threshold of the spiritual life stands
the dark and sinister figure of sin." But he has said this also:
"To realize the meaning of sin in feeling and in thought is
not the mark of a sick soul, but rather the sign of return to
spiritual health" (RR, 21).

I went to the man who was leading the group, and made to him a complete confession of all my past life (TBM, 166).

It is my own conviction that the truest counterpart of the Cross is the sharing of our sins. . . . It is easier to give what we have than what we are, our substance than ourselves, our labour than our personal sympathy, understanding and deeper feelings. The truth is that you can give your work, your money, your help, without its ever affecting your pride. When you share your real self, your pride goes down in a heap (GATY, 146–47).

We ought to find a person whom we can fully trust, who is spiritually sound and mature, and with such a person in full confidence to talk out our sins and problems through to the bottom. That will not only help in solving the immediate difficulty, but it may make the first real assault on our pride which is often so subtle that we do not know we have it (GATY, 150).

I believe . . . that a very frank sharing of one's inner struggles, temptations, and sins is the best thing here. One need not always go into detail, but sometimes one must (RR, 80–81).

The divine light reveals us to ourselves, and you can see people beginning to be spiritually awake as they grow in knowledge of themselves and of the real problems, the real sins, the real next steps that are necessary. It reveals other people to us, so that we are not fooled by them, not sentimental, for instance, about giving people money, not blind when psychological projection makes them critical of others about the very things that are true of themselves, and do not take their personal loyalty or appreciation *of us* as necessarily representing spiritual strength. It reveals to us the real needs of the world as moral and spiritual, not eco-

nomic or educational or medical or psychological, important as these are; and so gives us insight into what basically
needs to be done. It reveals to us that the world's great need
is, therefore, moral and spiritual recovery (GC, 47).

We know Him first as He purifies us by bringing convic-
tion of sin. If we face that we shall go on to know Him as
He warms us with the love of God and of one another which
He sheds abroad in our hearts (GC, 50).

For when we sit down alone and face ourselves as we
really are, we know that sin is a barrier between us and our
own best, and between us and God (RTW, 25–26).

I think that if you are honest you will agree with me that
the problem lies at our own door. . . . We must find out how
to go the rest of the way with our conversion.

Personally, I am quite clear how this must start. It must
start . . . by the sharing of these sins with another Christian
who has found his way a bit further than we have.

That has a Scriptural basis: "Confess your sins one to
another, and pray for one another that ye may be healed."
I would remind those of the Catholic inclination that it does
not say, "Confess your sins to a priest": and I would remind
those of the Protestant persuasion that it does not say, "Confess your sins to God only." It says very plainly, "Confess
your sins one to another." . . . I am equally convinced that
the Protestant notion of "confession to God only" ignores
the deep spiritual and psychological fact that we almost
always need a human hearer and witness to validate our
confession to God and make it *real to us.* Of course confession, in the absolute sense, is to God alone: but where
there is a human listener, confession is found to be both
most difficult and more efficacious. It is, as a matter of fact
and experience, a relatively uncostly thing to fall on our
knees and confess our sins to God—it should not be, and

perhaps would not be if we were closer to God and more sensitive to His will: but it is a very costly thing to speak out these things in the presence even of a human being we can trust; and, as a matter of fact, this is extraordinarily effective in making the first break to get away from sins. Almost every vital movement in spiritual history has made some use of this practice. Some of us prefer the word "sharing" to the word "confession": it has not quite such stiff and formal connotations. But whatever you call it, this experience is the same (CC, 38).

It is my conviction, and that of the Oxford Group with which I am associated, that detailed sharing should be made with one person only.... But we have known also the peculiar relief, having in it something closely akin to the grace of God, which comes when "the worst" is known to at least one other human soul, when someone else carries with us in sympathetic understanding the secret which lay like lead in our hearts.... You must yourself have been with someone in trouble when first they begin to ventilate their lapses, fears, prejudices, problems, sins, in an atmosphere of equality, sympathy, leisure and confidence, to know how simple and natural is the first step on the way back to spiritual health.

Of course, the mere externalizing of these difficulties does not banish them, though it is apt to banish emotional tension about them. They must next be gathered up in a new decision of the will and handed over to God in a new surrender (CC, 39–41).

The deepest realization we can have about ourselves is the realization that we are sinners. It is not a gloomy realization, far from it—unless you think that it is gloomy for sick people to want a doctor, or illiterate people to face the fact of their ignorance and want to learn. Being conscious of sin is just facing facts. And I find an appalling number of

Christian people who will say the General Confession, and say lustily in the Litany, "O God the Father of heaven, have mercy upon us, miserable sinners." But if you should say something which arouses their conscience a bit, they will say outside, "Oh well, I'm not so bad—guess I'm about as good as the next one." That is sometimes said in fun; but it generally proceeds out of a heart that has been dwelling upon its own superiority to the rest of mankind; and that is not a very Christian kind of meditation (IIBL, 31–33).

First, let us face it [sin] for a fact. Face the worst, in reality and in possibility. Don't brood on it, but face it. Are you afraid you have an incurable disease? Face it: get a thorough medical examination, be honest with yourself, and with those who have the right to know about you. Have you a dark spot of unbelief in your heart, so that your religion is a kind of wearing of a mask? Face it: admit it to yourself; remind yourself that it is not a final condition of mind, and expose yourself to searching religious experience, and to reading great books about religion. But don't fool yourself, be honest with yourself—and be especially honest as to the possible moral causes for unbelief in yourself, where sin hides faith from our eyes. Is there sin gnawing away at the vitals of your life? Face it: don't say you are not taking account of it, it's not a very big sin, you think it may wear off. Sin doesn't work that way. Look it in the face, and grapple with it, else you will carry it with you. Is your conscience pressing something upon you which you do not want to do? Face it: don't flinch and run away, for you cannot alter your deepest conviction, you can only obey it, or live a divided life (IIBL, 41–42).

Only God, therefore, can deal with sin. He must contrive to do for us what we have lost the power to do for ourselves. I hear men say that they will slough off sin in their onward march toward perfection. It seems to me childish. What will they do about the past, about willful wrong that has involved other people, and certain kinds of sin the whole consequences of which can never be humanly atoned for? What is going to make up for all "the days desolate and wasted years"? Nothing will do but for God Himself to stoop in ministrant condescension and good-will, and take these things upon Himself, and carry them for us (IIBL, 133).

And the thing to do with sin is to do what Nicodemus did: go and search out someone with whom we can talk privately and frankly. Tell them of these things and, with them as witness, give these sins and our old selves with them, to God. You say that you can do this alone with God; and I ask you, Have you succeeded in doing so? I said I was going to do that for years, but it never happened until I let a human witness come in on my decision. That is the "how" of getting rid of sin if you are in earnest about doing it at all: face it, share it, surrender it. Hate it, forsake it, confess it, and restore for it (NA, 58).

5

Willingness to Change and Humbly Seeking Rebirth

Step Six: Were entirely ready to have God remove all these defects of character.

Blessed are the pure in heart: for they shall see God.

Matthew 5:8

Repent ye therefore, and be converted, that your sins may be blotted out, when the times of refreshing shall come from the presence of the Lord.

Acts 3:19

Jesus answered and said unto him, Verily, verily, I say unto thee, Except a man be born again, he cannot see the kingdom of God.

John 3:3

Step Seven: Humbly asked Him to remove our shortcomings.

Humble yourselves in the sight of the Lord, and he shall lift you up.

James 4:10

Shoemaker believed there can be no vital religious experience—no return to companionship with God—without change. He emphasized willingness, which is to be characterized by obedience to what is known of God's will. To want to change, a person needs a personal conviction of sin. He must see the need to hate and forsake what he has been. He cannot see or enter the kingdom of God—cannot be born again—until he forsakes his old ways and accepts Jesus Christ as his Lord and Savior. The key is humbly asking God for help—turning to God and letting God impart His nature and effect the change.

It is the way of young-mindedness to treat one's spiritual defects as a problem, not a fate: and it is the happy province of God to keep men young in their minds, ready to meet a new call, willing to "go up higher" towards a better level of life and service (TBM, 36).

The rough edges, the small selfishnesses, the want of spiritual imagination, the disguised willfulnesses and independences had to go, and in the going pride got crucified more than once (TBM, 65).

Most of the misery of this world lies in divided hearts. We want to make the best of two worlds. We want God, but we want other things, too. The sense of conflict, the sense of sin, is really a well-placed danger signal, telling us that we are headed for trouble, perhaps nervous breakdown, because we are still two or more selves. And God made us to be one self, the self of His vision and His will for our life (GATY, 112).

For the last stand of self, in the righteous as in the sinner, is pride. We want some inner citadel, shut away from the influence of man or God, where we may cherish fine ideas about ourselves, nurse our hurt feelings which are usually only hurt pride, and make up to ourselves for the inadequate appreciation of an unjust world. There is no man or woman of us here who does not sin in that regard sometimes, and who does not need deliverance from it if God is ever to take the place of that self, and really reign in us. We can talk about humility as much as we like, and pray for it: but we shall not have it until our pride licks the dust. And the most common, the most natural, the most thorough way in which pride is made to lick the dust is by sharing (GATY, 147–48).

Our sins are those things which stand between us and Him; between us and our fellows. There is the downward drag of physical, instinctive appetite and desire, laziness, gluttony, impurity, the strange unsatisfyingness of satisfied flesh. He comes to them and wants to change them. But they are never the most serious sins. For back of them lies always a self that is out of harmony with God. The real place where sin begins is the place where the self breaks off from God (GATY, 160–61).

You can't change life, but you can change yourself. That is why it is anything but morbid to face your sins: it is the one healthy and hopeful thing any of us can possibly do. . . . Half our misery comes from our lying optimism about ourselves. There is positive joy in looking ourselves square in the face, and for the first time being honest with ourselves and with Him about ourselves. Hope and faith are born in

that moment. . . . We know that Christ Jesus came into the
world to save such as you and me,–to save us from the sins
we hate, to save us from the sins we love, to save us from
the sins we do not know, to save us from the one great, all-
inclusive sin of God-less, self-filled, self-directed, self-rid-
den lives (GATY, 166–67).

We begin to be ready to find God at the moment when
we know we must be reached down to by Him out of His
mercy, instead of reaching up to Him out of our spiritu-
ality. The aura of God is love, but the heart of God is holiness. Every man can feel the glory of that outgoing love, but
only the mercy of God's redemption allows us to approach
that holiness. Those who think themselves capable of bash-
ing through to immediate intimacy with God, those who
saunter unasked upon the premises of His holiness, simply
reveal their own spiritual conceit and immaturity (GATY,
172).

A man may actually be in touch with religious affairs for
years and never come to *a sense of personal sin*, which is
really the very door of religion; or connect in any way the
sin against which Christ spoke so vehemently and with
which He dealt, and still deals, so powerfully, with the moral
blunders of his own life (RR, 12).

A man I know naively remarked that he never sinned. I
suppose he meant that he never murdered anybody, nor got
intoxicated, nor stole money from his father. Would that sin
were always so patent as these! Probably not many with
money and leisure enough to pick up a book like this are
grossly immoral. But what of the spiritual meannesses which
Christ condemned so much more mercilessly than He condemned sins of overt passion? The things which fell us are
hypocrisy, white lies, insincerity, cruel thoughts, whispered
stories of gossip, hard, biting criticism, jealous longings,

pride, love of money and rivalry of other people's wealth that we would hardly admit to ourselves, curiosity, sly, lustful looks, vanity and the love of applause–all of them sins that we cherish behind an exterior so well maneuvered that no one would know we are not just as good as we look! We do not slay enemies, we just criticize them. We don't kill anybody, we just crush them with a sneer. Our adultery is within the heart. Our subtle, disguised selfishness takes refuge behind such a sheaf of checks and loveless generosity that we almost forget how hard our hearts really are. It is easy to see why Jesus sent the harlot away with a few cautionary but kindly and hopeful words, and then spoke fire to the Pharisees. It is easy to see why the drunken brutes of the gutter get a clean conversion, and we go on unconverted. For gross sin has this one great advantage: you can't tog it up in hypocrisy and make it pass for righteousness. It is the hidden sins, hidden by the wall of conventionality and decency with which we hedge ourselves round, that put us in the class with the Pharisee.

Sin is that forbidden thing which comes knocking at your heart for admission, which your inner self rejects. All that your best self vetoes is sin for you. As human consciences differ, one must grant a certain relativity in sin, so that what is right for one man may be wrong for another. But there is a sufficient body of undisputed wrong, so that this should not perplex anybody overmuch. And, besides, we are talking about "private, particular evils"–that is, yours and mine. Never a thought lodges within you, but you willed to let it lodge. It passed for approval before the inner eye. If it entered it was invited. If it went away, it was sent away. The hypocritical Pryer, in "The Way of All Flesh," complains of the fatal ambiguity of good and evil. But those who think simply, who through prayer learn to think as God thinks about evil, are not greatly perplexed. You can trust the inner voice if you are living in harmony with God.

If I am honest I will admit that in my very nature there is a rift, a cleavage, a division. It is Plato's white horse and black horse. It is Paul's flesh and spirit. It is Christ's God and mammon. There is eternal and unending conflict between them. And my soul is the battle field. The individual sins we commit flow from a disordered self. We might more safely ignore them were they not symptoms of a more deep-seated malady. They are the expression of a nature, a character, a will, which needs to be changed.

It is scarcely necessary to speak of the results of sin persisted in. It has "binding power, blinding power, multiplying power, deadening power." No other force can so unstring and despoil us. Its worst result is the increased capacity for sin, increased ease of sin, increased moral bluntness and irresponsibility. The wages of sin is death. Said a Russian soldier, "Now I fear neither God nor the devil. After I had stuck a bayonet into a man's stomach, it was as if something had fallen away from me."

But some reader has been longing to say, "But I am only following my impulses! Surely I am not depraved! Must I be always doing things I hate to do, and leaving what my whole being longs for? I loathe fighting with myself all the time. The conscientious type appalls me. The duty-driven are gloomy people. I long for something better than anything you have shown me. I long for freedom!" Yes, but remember, "freedom to live sanely and beautifully and serenely and well" (RR, 14–17).

There is an obvious truth that we cannot long be truly good without an experience of God; but there is a less obvious truth that we never can have an experience of God at all until our lives begin to be right. Only the pure in heart see God (GC, 45).

I talked to a young man who had had an experience of God, and then gone back on it: he did not see how he could ever "feel it" again, as he said. I told him if the willingness was there, God would give the feeling. He told me he was indifferent to people; and I told him if he surrendered that indifference to God, God would give him love for people. He simply said "All right," bowed his head and gave himself to God. Half an hour after I asked him whether he did not feel entirely different from what he had felt when he came in, and he said, "Yes, it's begun" (GC, 46).

The only answer I have ever found is a spiritual family that knows us better than we know ourselves, and by guided encouragement and guided criticism helps us to know ourselves and to get over our defects. Do we make that easy for people, or hard? How many of us can honestly say that we want to see ourselves as we really are? can say of our pride, "No man taketh it from me, but I lay it down of myself"? Be sure that one day life will "take it from us": there are not a few of us here this morning who have had it taken from us, and ground into the dust at one time or another. How much better to take up that inescapable cross of having to find out about ourselves in the end,–the whole, bitter, naked truth about our pride, our self-will, our duplicity,–how much better to take up that cross of our own volition, and let God, and people who are close to God, help us to face ourselves as we are, with a view to being different (GC, 105)?

I do not believe, my friends, that God sends trouble, or deliberately wills the trouble which comes upon the children of men. Much of it is of our own making, some is due to natural forces in the physical universe to which we belong, some of it I give up trying to understand. But I believe that God *uses* that trouble, turns it to good account, works it into the whole fabric of our lives, and gives meaning to it. . . . I believe that this person is nursing a sorrow for a kind of morbid joy which comes from the clinging to it. You cannot seek the meaning of a sorrow while you hug it to yourself, and will not give it to God to shed His light upon. You must let Him make something of it, or you have yourself been guilty of causing yourself injury, and cannot blame Him if you turn sour and grow hard. You have done it because you refused to find the meaning for yourself (RTW, 107).

Genuine humility cannot be attained by avoiding pride: it can only be attained by discovering gratitude. The truest humility in the world is that of the man who has been lifted up by God, carried above his sins, given peace for his pain and joy for his crying; and who, standing on the strong rock, thinks not of the security of his own position but of the mercy of God for putting him there. Yes, humility is a high place–a very high place indeed. There are human door-mats who feign humility but do not have it. They are cultivating it as a virtue: and the cultivation of humility as a virtue is almost a vice. Let them experience a great deliverance, or really know the salvation of God in their souls, and their humility will grow out of their sense of obligation and gratitude (RTW, 123).

What holds us back from faith and love and living for Christ and communion with God? Generally the thought of our utter unworthiness, which is another way of saying our sin. To each of us there is a familiar form of it, that besets and tortures and bedevils us: and which is the gateway to a train of discouragement and loneliness and more sin. And the reason we fail with the mastery of it is usually that we do not definitely give it up, or believe that we can give it up: but when we break it, keep the memory of its possibility in one corner of our minds, remembering that we can always go back to it. Let us claim for ourselves that great promise, in the fourteenth of Romans, "Sin shall have no more dominion over you" (RTW, 125–26).

I am going to consider with you to-day that quality in us which is the farthest of all from the Cross, and therefore needs spiritual treatment more than any of our moral ills, our pride. Jesus included it in the list of the things which come out of a man and defile the man. Those who made up the catalogue of the seven deadly sins put it where it belongs, at the head of the list. Pride is the deadliest sin of all. Of no other sins that I can recall is it specifically said in Scripture that God resists them: but of pride it is said twice in the New Testament, "God resisteth the proud."

Pride is "a high esteem of oneself for some real or imaginary merit or superiority" (IIBL, 26–27).

We all have regions and recesses in our minds where we carry about a tiny bit of pride, at the least; and a tiny bit of it is powerful, like a tiny bit of radium. It is the worst thing in us, worse than uncleanness, worse than irritability, worse than dishonesty. Our pride is on the other side of the world of our souls from God. God hates it, I believe God fears it, as nothing else in us; for it is the quickest, the most certain to cut us off from Him of all that comes between us.

This is the fact. What is the cure?

The antidote for pride is not humility, but gratitude. Humility is still struggling with one's own attitude: gratitude has found something without, in the presence of which to forget oneself and bow down in thankfulness. Pride may hide unseen in humility; but pride is gone out of thankfulness. Do you remember when the apostles came back from an evangelistic campaign, and Jesus was asking them about it; and in their enthusiasm of success, their pride of spiritual influence, they said, "Lord, even the demons are subject unto us through Thy Name." It was a danger signal, but Jesus did not say, "You must be humble." He said, "In this rejoice not that the demons are subject unto you: but rather rejoice that your names are written in heaven." Do not marvel at what God has done *through* you, for you may wind up merely marvelling at you: but marvel at what God has done *for* you, for He has had compassion on you and is saving you unto eternal life. The inspiration of His flashing answers to their revealed needs wants no further witness than its own inherent and self-luminous truth (IIBL, 33–34).

For humility is not a thing which can be cultivated directly. A man who tries to be humble may be as proud as Lucifer underneath: we all know of people who are proud of being humble. But genuine humility is a by-product,–a by-product, I suspect, of thankfulness. If you can make a man thankful for almost anything you have gone a long way toward making him humble (IIBL, 162).

6

Reconciliation and Setting Things Right

Step Eight: Made a list of all persons we had harmed, and became willing to make amends to them all.

Therefore if thou bring thy gift to the altar, and there rememberest that thy brother hath ought against thee; leave there thy gift before the altar, and go thy way; first be reconciled to thy brother, and then come and offer thy gift.

Matthew 5:23–24

Step Nine: Made direct amends to such people wherever possible, except when to do so would injure them or others.

If a man say, I love God, and hateth his brother, he is a liar: for he that loveth not his brother whom he hath seen, how can he love God whom he hath not seen?

1 John 4:20

Thou hypocrite, first cast out the beam out of
thine own eye; and then shalt thou see clearly to
cast out the mote out of thy brother's eye.

Matthew 7:5

Shoemaker made much of the idea that the Christian
life involves a current of electricity which runs through God,
ourselves, and other people; and that a block anywhere in
the circuit will put a stop to the current. Living in touch with
God, having a successful contact and relationship with Him,
is inextricably bound up with human relationships. We cannot stay in touch with God without righting the human relationships. This is the law of love in action. We love because
He first loved us.

In order to leave nothing undone in the attempt to make
things right with people I had wronged, I wrote fourteen
letters of confession of specific wrong. Without exception,
they all forgave me and wished me well in my new life (TBM,
166).

For most people there is wrapped up in the decision to
surrender to God the necessity to right all wrongs with men,
and it generally means a specific wrong of act or attitude
toward somebody in particular. This is the hurdle of
restitution.

I knew a clergyman once who used to lose his temper
with his curate, and by way of restitution he would send a
parcel of magazines to the curate's wife. That indirectly
acknowledges the wrong, but certainly is inadequate as
restitution.

If our relation to God is real, it involves love and honesty in all our human relations also. You cannot carry that
resentment or hate or social dislike toward anyone in your
heart, and then expect to live in touch with God. I know

heaps of nominal Christians who wonder why they do not have divine guidance, and the joy of real faith; but over in the corner of their minds and memories, motionless but not dead, is an old resistance against someone. Vaguely we know we are in for a difficult letter, or visit. But we put it off. We really refuse that hurdle, and want to go on in our course.

But it will not be put off. That is simply the next fence, and it has got to be jumped, or we stay just where we are. What reception we find in the other person is not our responsibility—only that we go to him in love and in honesty and clear any wrong on our side. If you know that a hurdle awaits you now like that, I beg you to say to-day, "With the help of my God I shall leap over the wall, and establish that relation so far as in me lies."

There is another hurdle that will soon loom before us. If we begin to live Christ's way of life with any sincerity, the family will have to know about it. If we have given our lives to Him so far as we can, it means our values and purposes are different, and that will affect our daily decisions and attitudes.

No atmosphere is so likely to frustrate us as the familiar atmosphere of home, and no group of people is so likely to keep us pigeon-holed in the same old category we used to belong in as the family. Sometimes they are definitely antagonistic toward a challenging change in the life of one of their members. Perhaps as often we are self-conscious and create the difficulty for ourselves by expecting them to be unsympathetic. It is a real hurdle to make restitution where it is necessary at home, and to tell the family simply of our new-found life. We need very sure guidance about how it shall be done. All our most profound emotions are involved, and we shall tend to say too much, or to say it either dogmatically or fearfully.

Unless our lives match our words in time to come, they will lose all weight and effect. We are quite right in thinking that living is more important than talking within the family. But talking is part of living, it is living put in ready and transmissible form. We must make the plunge which makes it natural for us to talk about our faith with the family when it is guided. That means somewhere the jumping of a hurdle of honesty with them. We shall need the kind of prayer from which we rise saying, "With the help of my God I shall leap over the wall that has kept us separated from one another in the family, as to our innermost convictions and concerns" (GATY, 87–89).

It is natural to set things right when the heart is moved with a sense of its own sin; it is next to impossible when the sense is all of the other fellow's sin (RR, 19).

By obedience God gets us where we begin fulfilling His plan. For instance: here is a man guided to make restitution for his resentment against some of his own family. If he does it fully, he reestablishes relationships with them. That opens spiritual opportunity so that they may also be changed. . . . No one can be impervious to the influence of absolute honesty spoken with absolute love (GC, 12).

Will you go through the needed adjustments to make your home a source of true spiritual power? You may have to apologize to someone. You may have to see possibilities in someone in whom you have only seen a block (GC, 89).

He has got to lay down his detachment and pride, share his resentments and self-righteousness with his wife, create a different home by being different himself (GC, 108).

While the old wrong itself may have ceased to do any harm, as a needle may become embedded somewhere in the body and be harmless, the pride which will not share the wrong is still a present fact; and the only way to break the pride is to share the wrong (CC, 41).

The first necessity is to get straight with all other people: those we have written off our list, those we dislike and disapprove of, those with whom we come into daily but not always wholly loving and honest contact. The first thing I had to do was to write a letter to someone in my own family, and clear up a long-standing resentment. Some of you have got to straighten out your income tax, or pay your bills in the village, or apologize to the neighbor over the fence, or to your cook for your bad disposition. What is the use of a lot of pious flimflam on Sundays about "love divine all loves excelling, joy of heaven to earth come down," when there are people who hate religion and mock God because of the lives we live day by day? You can't be straight with God and not be straight with people (NA, 60).

A lot of us wonder how we can make religion real to other people. We have a son or daughter, we have a neighbor who gets drunk, we know a couple thinking about divorce. What can influence them? We run vainly to a psychiatrist or a minister, who may or may not have any answer for them. What about beginning with a problem of our own that has been solved? We have tried advice, preaching, lugging them off to church, and that has not worked. Let's try a little sharing of our faults, instead of theirs! In the case of someone we don't like, let's begin sharing our faults in the situation. That is what Christ meant by turning the other cheek, and it's only the most supreme common sense (NA, 61).

Have you thought of leisure, not as a holiday, but as a God-given opportunity to go to work for Christ? I am thinking about a middle-aged businessman, retired, with plenty to live on. He said that he was unhappy, and blamed it on his wife. Now one of the qualities of being really "different"

today is the quality of looking at our own sins before we
begin looking at other people's. Some people have been
praying for that man. Some time ago I got in touch with him
and had a talk with him. He began to blame his wife for his
misery. I told him he had plenty of sins to begin on in his
own life, and one of them was his resentment towards her.
He gave his life to God, wrote a letter of honest confession
and restitution to his wife, and has begun to find that God
has a will for his otherwise empty days. He wants to go to
work for God and give away what he has found (NA, 72–73).

If we are to find it [a better relationship], we must begin
by admitting freely the defects of the one which exists, and
stop muddling along with it. Each person must face the
need for a change of mind and heart: and one side must do
the difficult work of making a beginning. We must remember that, no matter how adamant the other person may
seem, God can change a personality. We must shake off our
old stiff thoughts about the relation, the discouragement
and despair. We must begin praying to God, and letting Him
through prayer convince us that He can do something.

Then one day we must, in an atmosphere of frankness
and love on our part, share our own wrong in the situation.
The matter has got to be aired, fully and unevasively. It is
the "truth that shall make you free." You may feel it right to
say what you believe is the cause of the wrong in the relationship: but you will not attach guilt except to yourself.
Even if the fault is nine parts on the other side, and one on
yours, confess the one, not the nine! If you play for position, or try to justify yourself, a bad matter will be made
worse. Now you may feel guided to wait for this honest session until the other person first sees a spiritual change in
you. Some time ago a married woman talked with me. She
had gone off with another man, and been advised by a clergyman not to tell her husband of it. We first made sure of
her own surrender to Christ: and then I advised that she

wait till her husband found in her the new spirit; and then as she was led, she would one day tell him. She did that, and she told me that he had faced the whole matter with her in full sympathy and understanding. The lie would always have been a barrier: premature sharing might have caused trouble; but only good has come of what she did. We must share our own fault, and take the possibly unhappy consequence of criticism, instead of understanding, in all patience: nothing else will so convict the other person ultimately of his or her wrong as the way we face honestly all our own sin (CF, 25–26).

7

Walking with God in Daily Life

Step Ten: Continued to take personal inventory and when we were wrong promptly admitted it.

... by God's help, I can leap a wall.
Psalm 18:29 (Moffatt)

Speak; for thy servant heareth.
1 Samuel 3:10

... speaking the truth in love, we may grow up into him in all things, which is the head, even Christ.
Ephesians 4:15

Shoemaker saw progress in Christian life as mastering the new situations that come up before us like hurdles. The initial hurdle is deciding whether to run the race at all. The next is overcoming unbelief and dividedness in our hearts with God's help. Then there are the hurdles of daily surrender and continued righting of wrongs. At all times what is required is an honest facing up to the struggle. Then, also, we need to seek the help of God, expectantly listening for His voice. Shoemaker felt that "speaking the truth in love" is the basic principle of spiritual fellowship.

Through the long Quiet Times which were recommended, I discovered four things which needed putting right in my life:

1. There was one person who had wronged me whom I would not forgive.
2. There was a restitution which I would not make.
3. There was a doubtful pleasure which I would not give up.
4. There was a sin in the long past which I would not confess.

When these were straightened out, I not only came into new power and release, but for the first time began to get daily guidance which I knew could be relied and acted upon, because my own life was disciplined. Almost daily new surrenders have to be made, but I can honestly say that nothing is left standing between God and myself, or other people and myself. Consequently, I entered upon a period of radiant joy and peace, and life is just wonderfully full and overflowing (TBM, 92).

There is the need for re-dedication day by day, hour by hour, by which progressively, in every Quiet Time, the contaminations of sin and self-will are further sloughed off (for they do have a way of collecting) and we are kept in fresh touch with the living Spirit of God. A further surrender is needed when and whenever there is found to be something in us which offends Christ, or walls us from another. We shall need, in this sense, to keep surrendering so long as we live (CC, 81).

8

The Guidance of God

Step Eleven: Sought through prayer and meditation to improve our conscious contact with God *as we understood Him,* praying only for knowledge of His will for us and the power to carry that out.

Give ear to my words, O LORD, consider my meditation. Hearken unto the voice of my cry, my King, and my God: for unto thee will I pray. My voice shalt thou hear in the morning, O LORD; in the morning will I direct my prayer unto thee, and will look up.

Psalm 51:1–3

Lord, what wilt thou have me to do?

Acts 9:6

Shoemaker regarded the guidance of God as a paramount factor in the Christian's establishment of a relationship with God and becoming God-conscious. He advocated prayer, Bible study, listening for leading thoughts, and worship in the church itself as vital. Originally, he was a strong advocate of the "Morning Watch," but later subscribed to the phrase "Quiet Time," since it allows for communion with God throughout the day. He believed that God's general will can be found in the Bible and God's particular will through application of the principle of John 7:17. He held that the important thing in prayer is not to change the will and mind of God, but to find them.

The beginning of a daily habit of Quiet Time is perhaps the crucial point in maintaining the new life (TBM, 167).

The most important part of prayer is not what we say, but what we hear—not what we do, but what God does (TBM, 184).

Let a man cultivate that time alone with the living God day by day, refusing his newspaper before he has had his Quiet Time, and his conversion has at least one good leg to stand on (TBM, 185).

I do not say that every unusual thought which comes into our minds is God speaking: but I do say that He speaks to us much more often than we admit, and that He is always trying to make contact with us through God-given ideas. These will be more trustworthy as we become more disciplined, trained in Christ, instructed in His written Word. . . . Give yourself humbly to Him, and ask Him to give Himself to you (GATY, 52–53).

Whatever be one's theories about prayer, two things stand: man will pray as long as God and he exist, and the spiritual life cannot be lived without it. . . . People need to pray, and they pray.

But it is an art—the art of discerning God's will—and one must learn it. For prayer is more than primitive awareness of the supernatural; for us Christians it is the communing of children with Father. Sin will ever be its greatest hindrance, for sin rises up as a cloud between ourselves and God, and makes our companionship a mockery. And in the same way obedience to the Voice which speaks in prayer must ever be the condition of hearing that Voice again. We ask for what we need, remembering that the essence of prayer is not childish asking for gifts, but the eternal quest for the disposition of God towards the ways of our life. And we are praying best when we come, quite empty of request, to bathe ourselves in His presence, and to "wait upon Him" with an open mind, concerned far more with His message to us than with anything we can say to Him. And as one grows into the longing love of God for men, intercession becomes more and more a necessity, first because we can't help it, knowing somehow that the best we can ever do for those we love is to bear them up before God, and also to seek some hint from God of what He yearns to do for them through us. The prayer of confession and for forgiveness is perhaps the deepest, best prayer of all, and the one which we shall need most often if God gives us an acute sense of sin.

However necessary it be, prayer is seldom easy. "I have followed my *own* will so *prayerfully* and intensely, that I do not know how to *find* another will," wrote my friend. Sometimes the impression is vague, and we are not sure it is from God. Or there seems to be no impression at all. Now we should not seek emotional corroboration for every spiritual effect produced by God upon us, and He often pours power into us when we "feel" nothing. Very clear leadings come seldom to most people. Some of us are too sinful or too stupid to be guided by revelation, we must be guided by necessity. And God is constantly using persons or events to direct us when our wills are at too great discord with His for us to be guided directly. There is a temple in Kyoto with 500 images of the goddess of mercy, having in all 33,333 hands. This would be a faint representation of God's desire to come into our lives, to guide us, to help us. Trusting Him, then, we must pray on, for we can do no other. And if we be faithful, we shall soon find that the reality of the experience of prayer far outweighs the reality of the questionings which make us doubt it.

Romain Rolland says, "Only the mean of spirit never need to pray."

One word more about the time of prayer. Some find occasion for intercessions at noon, most of us pray regularly morning and night, and briefly through the day. If the reader will pardon a personal testimony, the time when the writer began to have a hitherto unknown power in his own life, and some slight influence spiritually in the lives of others, coincides exactly with the time when he changed the chief time of prayer from the last thing at night to the first thing in the morning. I plead again for the keeping of the "Morning Watch"—coming fresh to God with the day's plans unmade, submitting first our spirits and then our duties to Him for the shedding of his white light upon both. "To steam full-speed through icebergs is irreligious. To start the day without one thought of our Maker is to invite catastrophe" (RR, 63–66).

I used to wonder whether "praying in the Spirit" meant some special form of ecstasy; I believe now it means praying as God directs and leads one to pray. Have you ever had God tell you to pray for somebody, for an event? That kind of prayer is cooperation with Him; the old kind of prayer was just the "gimmes." The one thing antichrist cannot stand against is a man in touch with the living God. Each of us is actually in touch with an infinity of good, or an infinity of evil. God controls our minds, or Satan does. Real prayer is being where God can talk to you (GC, 32).

Ordinarily the Voice of divine guidance is not audible, it speaks in our thoughts. But there are times when that Voice speaks so clearly, so insistently, so personally to us that, while it does not sound in the ears of our head, it may sound in the ears of our mind. And when that call is to a deeper giving of ourselves to God, to a true repentance, to reconciliation with our fellows, we cannot doubt that the Voice is the Voice of God. When God wants to take the initiative with humanity, He speaks directly to the heart of some open human spirit. You do not hear the rumblings of millions of ether waves through hundreds of radio stations coming at you altogether: you hear one radio station through your one radio. God sends over one intelligible thought to one ready person. Sometimes we human beings get ourselves and our generation into such an inextricable mess that we literally cannot move with any hope. Only God can do something with us. For individuals the next step is, as Sokolsky says, the task of learning to pray again, to commune with God, to listen, because what God has for us in prayer is more important than what we have for Him. . . . How many of us, I wonder, really believe that God is more eager to help us in our daily living than we are to have His help? that for every question He has an answer, for every problem a solution, for every need a supply? So often we want that answer, solution and supply at once and in our own way, and are unwilling to be guided in the intermediate steps through which God must lead us before He may choose to grant them to us. God is always taking the initiative, always broadcasting. He is in touch with everyone just as much as we let Him be. Religion is not a creation of ours, it is a reception. God initiates in all true matters of the Spirit. He moves on men's hearts and in their minds (GC, 114–15).

"Speak, Lord; for thy servant heareth." God's initiative is grace and guidance. Man's initiative in response is surrender to God. That begins with an act of the will by which we hand ourselves over to Him. Sometimes people do that once, and then it does not hold because there is no renewal of it in daily life. Every time we listen to the Voice of God, every time we close what we have to say to God with that prayer, "Speak, Lord: for thy servant is listening," we renew our own surrender to God. It is the answer for continuing a spiritual experience which we have begun. The secret of all divine guidance is to be willing to obey what God tells us. His Voice becomes plain to all who are ready to obey. Are we ready? Have we got far enough to know that man's plans fail, that God's plans adulterated and modified by man's plans fail, that only God's plans succeed? Is our obedience to God a leap, or a concession? Is our daily life a series of struggles between ourselves and God, or have we got to the place where we take God's word without talking back (GC, 115–16).

I believe enormously in the possibility of a guided life. . . . Conversion is the beginning, not the ending, of an experience of God. . . . I believe God meant each one of us to experience a fresh and personal relationship to Him which becomes creative and original. Many situations in my life are not covered by the Sermon on the Mount. I need special guidance and illumination. . . .

What infinite possibilities of learning the will of God, through communion with Him, may lie ahead of us, who can dare to imagine (RTW, 14–15)?

And then there is another high place of Christian experience. It is the height a man reaches when *prayer becomes the climate of his life*. Not a ritual, not a habit, not a last resort, but a climate wherein a man's soul draws breath. One comes increasingly to believe in the reality of a spiritual kingdom, as high above the animal kingdom as the animal is above the inanimate—a kingdom with its own laws which supersede the laws that science understands in the two lower kingdoms. When a human soul lives continually in that kingdom, the common events of life are seen in a glow of significance, coincidences turn into Providences, frustrations into opportunity, and miracle becomes the order of the day. There is a higher ether which if a man breathe, all his normal gifts are lifted into super-human power, as unlettered men were empowered to write the most immortal books in the world. . . . And in that kingdom, the communication of the will of God to our finite minds becomes, in the truest sense, natural: it is expected, we are quiet enough to hear, and obedient enough to understand; our wills slip over into God's will and become one with it (RTW, 124–25).

I began to see that the point about prayer was to ask Him to show me His plan—so that listening became more important than talking. And so the effective "how" of keeping in touch with the living God, renewing the decision of surrender day by day, is a daily time alone with Him, waiting for His direction, writing down in words what He says to us, and carrying them out. That is the vertical dimension of religion (NA, 59).

What Eli said to Samuel that day is the last word in spiritual advice: " . . . thou shalt say, Speak, Lord; for thy servant heareth." There is active faith, and the listening attitude, and the patience which waits for the emergence of God's plan, all wrapped in one. If there be any such thing as a recipe for being in touch with God, it is contained in those inspired words. They do not preclude ordinary prayer, but they supersede it. They do not overlook man's part in religion, which is receptive cooperation—"thy servant heareth"; but they put first God's part, in time and in importance. They are the kernel of surrender, the climate of prayer, and the essence of living faith. There are no words in the world that we can better carry constantly in our hearts, and in the framed but soundless prayers of our lips, as we move about all day in the ways of the world, or, like Samuel, lie upon our couch at night. "Speak, Lord; for thy servant heareth." Why, it almost seems as if Eli had compressed the whole core of religion into six words! And in that God-given attitude, Samuel both validated his previous guidance and prepared himself for more (NA, 83–84).

And we need to know that guidance is not for our private comfort, or even illumination, but that by it God means to touch some actual human situation that needs to be touched and cured: we cannot be or keep in touch with God Whom we have not seen, if we are not living creatively, lovingly, realistically, with men whom we have seen (NA, 86).

Are you in touch with God? . . . Are you still back in the doldrums of wondering whether it is possible to be in touch with God, instead of knowing by now that all difficulties lie in yourself and are of your own making, and that when you are open God is ready to be in touch with you? Is the experience of being in touch with God growing, so that He can depend upon you to carry out His will, especially in difficult situations which require maturity, insight and judgment? Is being in touch with God lifting you above the defeats which have kept you down–the moods, the signs of temper and irritation, the ever-present willfulness which only God can destroy (NA, 87)?

9

The Experience of Christ–Passing It On, Living Love

Step Twelve: Having had a spiritual awakening as the result of these steps, we tried to carry this message to alcoholics, and to practice these principles in all our affairs.

Ye must be born again.

John 3:7

He that loseth his life for my sake shall find it.

Matthew 10:39

Seek ye first the kingdom of God . . . and all these things shall be added unto you.

Matthew 6:33

This is life eternal, that they might know thee the
only true God, and Jesus Christ, whom thou hast
sent.

John 17:3

Ye shall receive power, after that the Holy Ghost
is come upon you: and ye shall be witnesses unto
me.

Acts 1:8

Such as I have give I thee.

Acts 3:6

The greatest of these is love.

1 Corinthians 13:13 NIV

Shoemaker was convinced that God-consciousness
comes when self is surrendered and is replaced by the
guidance of the Holy Spirit. He was very clear, however,
that "you have to give it away to keep it." He pointed out
that there is no more empowering habit in the lives of those
who seek to live the Christ-life than "fishing for men," as
Jesus called it. And he was equally clear on the importance
of living by the principles of 1 Corinthians 13.

It seems to me clear that the best way to help people concerning religion today is not only to present convincing,
objective reasons to their minds, but also to show them pictures of those who are finding rich spiritual experiences,
pictures which will rather fire their imaginations than per-
suade their minds (TBM, 9).

If I was to come up against crying need in human lives
and have an answer for that need, the needs of my own life
must be met first, down deep where the world does not see.
You can't give what you haven't got. It struck me that too

many people were missed entirely by good souls who helped superficially with good advice, sympathy and money. I had had help like this, and it had never cured me, and I knew such things never cured anybody else. The men who did the most for me were the men who cared enough to give themselves, their inner lives and experiences, and helped me to face my own true self and carried me through to a solution. There is all the difference in the world.

Since my surrender I have repeatedly tried the way of compromise in my own life, and each time any power I might have had in other people's lives has disappeared. With these temporary deflections, new issues arise, new surrenders must be made which bring new release and power. I cannot possibly face a life given to the ministry on any other basis than that of literally dying daily to sin. I have got to be willing to do what others did for me, turn my life inside out where it will help anybody else, and to make sure of my own cleansing experience of Jesus Christ day by day, so that a fellow in need can come to me and find through me a real answer to his troubles–a regenerating experience of Jesus Christ. This may bring me into conflict with the average idea of parish work, perhaps, but I do want to put first things first. It is easy to get side-tracked into a life of intense parish activity, with not much sense of direction, and only meagre results. But Jesus Christ came into the world to save sinners, and I believe that that is still His commission to those who have given themselves to Him without reservation.

Ultimately there is no answer to critics and objectors but the old, pragmatic, New Testament measuring-rod of spiritual fruits (TBM, 107–108).

Any Thursday night after the meeting you will see little knots of people talking together in various corners of the hall–some chatting lightly about "what a wonderful meeting it was," but others down at rock-bottom deciding the issues of life. The Sensitive Soul is often the human centre of one of these groups of two or three. Gloriously and at long last, he has gotten out of himself. His life is free and gay for the first time. The old moods, of course, come back momentarily, but he knows what to do with them. Intelligently, sympathetically he is living his life out into other lives. His own problems and their solution form the basis and ground-work of his message. His understanding and sympathy have been distilled out of his old sufferings transfigured by a growing experience of Jesus Christ (TBM, 162).

Fellowship in a group of believers, each sustaining the other, honest sharing, are needful if the experience is not to die in isolation, or, if it persists, be warped through individualism. But one of the chief needs is that this life should express itself in the lives of others. As Frank Buchman often says, "No man can maintain a growing experience of Jesus Christ whose life does not have an intelligent expressional activity." To take a life lighted at the fire of Christ, and expect to feed that fire by cool, humanitarian efforts is to court failure: to put a man such as we have been describing to teaching boys to play basketball, or raising money for a hospital, or working in a settlement where religion cannot be mentioned, and to think that thereby his spiritual life will be sustained, is to help him back into the abyss. He needs *spiritual* service, he needs to be helped to give to other men what he has been given. Apart from what it will mean to them, let us think now of what it will mean to him. One needs hardly labour the great point contained in the remark of Novalis [quoted by Carlyle in *Sartor Resartus*], "It is certain my belief gains quite infinitely the moment I can convince another mind thereof."

And so, a recently converted man was taken into a little group of men and women who were to spend that summer travelling and working for Christ in many different centres, speaking informally to invited people in houses, and working with individuals. All the values of continuance would be thus conserved. In his times of critical temptation, he would be surrounded by those who knew of his struggles and would understand and sustain him. His questions could be answered, his moods of rebellion and slipping, bound to come to us all, could be dealt with. But chiefly he could begin an active witness under the direction of those who knew how to do it (TBM, 167–69).

People that have been converted need study, but it must be *live* study, that feeds their imaginations and helps them in working for others. They need prayer, but it must be living prayer in which things take place: guidance is adventurous, even when it refers to home-drudgery or church responsibilities, and it feeds the fires of faith. They need worship, but they will find that out down the trail a bit much better than they will at the beginning. Don't smother a new convert with all the safeguards the church has found valuable as an offset to enthusiasm, or you'll probably put out the fire altogether!

Now, the greatest help in continuance, next to vital Quiet Times, is a sharing fellowship. It must be made up of like-minded people. It may begin with you and one other person. I made a fatal mistake in forming our first group at Calvary, by throwing the invitation open to everybody: about thirty came, and I did all the talking because none of them had had a vital experience, and after three months, I knocked the thing in the head and began over again. The group must begin with converted people. You want time for united Quiet. You want time for sharing up-to-date. And you will talk about working with other people. As others are won, they will be brought into the group, and occasionally some may be brought in before they are won, provided you are sure they won't run away with the meeting, and that there are enough people there who are really won to set and maintain the level of reality. Gradually enough people are won to ensure real testimonies and to follow any unreal talk from a newcomer by a strong, guided witness. These meetings, held perhaps weekly, are kept fresh and vital by the testimonies of new people, and by new experiences of those who have been won. There is no place here for the dreary repetition of stale spiritual history, and while you may occasionally draw a shouter, or a quoter of texts and "lovely thoughts," they will usually find the pace a little rapid for them and not come back. If they persist in spoiling your meetings, you may have to tell them to stay away: but we have only had occasion to do that once in three and a half years of our Thursday evening meetings, and once I had to haul a man down for silliness while he was speaking. In such a group the masks are off. People are themselves, and if they pretend to be anything else, they do not fool you for long. Here all the difficulties of the further stages of the journey can be faced frankly together, the dry times, the times of returning temptation, of discouragement, of bafflement over how to win somebody. But the genius of maintaining such a group lies in keeping people moving forward all the time, sharing honestly with somebody right along, and trying to win others: and the genius of conducting such a group lies in ease, naturalness, laughter, freedom from strain, and above all running openness to God's Holy Spirit to tell you what to do next. In course of time it may be inevitable that the meeting should be open to all. Through honest testimony which often touches the concrete details of life, others see their own difficulties mirrored, and find not only that they are not alone in their struggle, but also that there is a solution in a real experience of Jesus Christ. A group like this should raise up leadership from within itself. One man I know, when he accepted another call, left behind him in his parish a group of lay-people which has continued unabated in his absence: lives continue to be changed as a result of the work of that group (TBM, 189–91).

The ambition to achieve something in this world is a part of living; but if we are growing, if we are maturing out of childhood and becoming spiritual adults, there is a steady shifting of the point of gravity from our own part in that achievement, to the achievement itself, while self recedes. There is a strong element of impatience in the temptation to cut a sudden figure. A dramatic forecast is very different from a steady accomplishment. We ministers and the Christian church at large have not been free from this temptation, and we have often succumbed to it. We have sent forth brave prospectuses about what we intended to bring to pass, thousands of people touched, and thousands of dollars raised, and spiritual awakening set on its way. It is more impressive to stay off the pinnacles of prophecy, and keep on the solid ground of steady achievement (GATY, 137).

One of the normal human instincts after a decisive conversion is the craving for companionship, someone with whom to share the mysteries of the great secret, "someone who understands" (RR, 67).

Every single life that is in touch with God and with other people on an honest and loving basis is convincing on an individual scale; and, as all of us start there, it is of the greatest importance. When you see a person happy who was unhappy, victorious who was defeated, living by a plan who was aimless, you know he has found something (GC, 13).

The people I know who have been purified and warmed and illumined by the fire Christ sends into the world, are also empowered to accomplish what no other people I know accomplish. They get the message of Christ into high places and low, where ordinarily it never comes. Their influence far outreaches their worldly position, academic training or human personalities. Men give up their old ways, their old

values, when they meet them. People indifferent to God
begin talking about God, turn to God, listen to God.

A relatively small company of such people is already
becoming the salt that sweetens the world, the leaven that
penetrates it, the light that illumines it. That first Church of
Christ was like that. What is spiritual power? It is not
numerical importance. It is not political pull. It is not mystical capacity. Spiritual power is influence which leads to
life-changing. That was spiritual power in the beginning and
it is spiritual power now (GC, 49).

Touching lives one by one is fascinating business, and
involves some of the most rewarding and beautiful human
relationships that can possibly arise (RTW, 16).

Share your trouble. I do not mean share it for the relief
it brings to you to talk about it, for that may be, after a time,
a very selfish thing to do. I mean, share it where it will create an atmosphere in which someone else in trouble can
share that trouble with you, so that *they* may find relief.
There are gushing people, moist with piety and dripping
with sentimentality, who find dissipation in unburdening
their troubles on others—plainly they must learn how to be
unselfish with sorrow, so that they do not force it on all, but
also do not withhold it from those whom it will help. The
sun alone can set free a ship caught in frozen ice-fields; and
you may keep a heart from breaking if you can start an ice-
floe. The sharing of trouble which is for our own relief is
selfish and sentimental, the sharing which builds a bridge
across into the heart of another is one of God's benedic-
tions let into the world (RTW, 105–106).

I should like always to live in the high places of *love*. Love
that allows nobody to stand outside its view, builds no arti-
ficial fences between people, sees men's hearts and not their
clothes or their colour, and looks on them somewhat as

God looks on them. Love that is never uncomfortable in the presence of incompatibles, but with ingenuity brings together into fellowship divers kinds of people who would usually not understand each other, love which is a great reconciler of those whom the crusty custom of the world has divided. Love that rejoices in the success of those who are our rivals, is fair to the truth of those who are our critics, is patient of those who willfully misunderstand us.

Love that is brave enough to call sin sin, and to include all men under sin: and then to refuse to believe that there is a soul anywhere that cannot be saved. Love for those that irritate us, foolishly take our time, needlessly harry us about trifles, are stupid about taking a hint. Love that always sees people and situations as they lie in the mind of God, big with potentiality, no matter what the situation be. I am convinced that love like that will wear some of us out, and tax us beyond human power: it crucified Christ, but it set going a new force in human life (RTW, 122).

I should like always to make an *impression for Christ,* and not for myself, upon every life I meet. There are lives in the world obviously possessed. One feels in them both the constraint and the liberty of a great Other, with them at all times. That impression would be made often by words, for what a man loves most, that he talks about. But it will be made, too, by the subtlest attitudes, by the things he reads and doesn't read in the newspapers, by the books on his table, by the recreation he chooses, by the way he talks to the telephone operator, and says good-morning to the elevator man in his office. You know as well as I do that there are people who live that way twenty-four hours in the day, and they are not saccharine and effusive people, they are as often quiet and restrained people (RTW, 123–24).

What really gets people at the outset? Only one thing—experience told with humour and enthusiasm. The ordinary processes of friendship must build sufficient confidence at first, but the first gun to fire is a piece of news. It will probably be the story of your own experience of Christ as you feel guided to tell it, adapted all the while to the sort of person you are talking to. It might be the story of someone else whose situation is more nearly parallel than your own. The Gospel was originally "news," not "views" (CC, 75).

When a person finds Him fully, they have a message about Him for other people (CC, 87).

The fruit of Christianity is service, but the root of it is being in touch with the living God, which brings spiritual power into life. One of the places where that power overflows is in service. Our modern world wants to take a desirable fruit of Christianity and say that it is Christianity itself. This is not the service which overflows from a relationship with God through Christ; this is a substitute for that relationship. Humanity then becomes our god, and service our religion (NA, 13).

So many come to us today with intellectual arguments in their minds and on their lips: they can't believe this, or they won't go on till that is settled. How do you meet them—with attempts at proof and argument? or are you stocked with miracles, miracles you have seen in others, miracles you have heard from others, miracles that have happened to you and through you? One argument in religion is about as good as another: but an experience beats any argument. Men run from your arguments about God, they will not listen to your elaborate explanations; but when you tell them what life was without God, and then tell them what it is with Him, their hearts, as John Wesley said, are "strangely warmed," and their minds also are strangely persuaded (NA, 28).

There is something more than helping people meet the immediate crisis of their need: there is changing them, taking advantage of their situation to let them learn the power and reality of God (NA, 71).

10

Shoemaker's Christian Lifelines

Sam was called by his associate, Rev. Irving Harris, a "Bible Christian." His teaching and writing spoke from the deep belief that God has revealed his general will in the Scriptures and that a person can learn God's particular will for him by expressing a willingness to obey, and then acting in obedience to God's general will. Shoemaker spoke much about the nature of a real spiritual awakening. He felt that it involves prayer, conversion, witnessing, and fellowship. He said that the individual who seeks God first through prayer, Bible study, listening, and worship will have God's will revealed to him. Moreover, "where God guides, He provides"; and whoever obeys God will experience the power and presence of God in his life. Then the task is to witness and fellowship with other believers. Shoemaker's thoughts should sound familiar both to Christians and to members of Alcoholics Anonymous.

For the heart of spiritual merriment is gratefulness, not accomplishment: it is the blessedness of God's mercy, not satisfaction with one's own character (TBM, 83).

There is something invaluable and unique about the depth of fellowship on a guided basis of Christian living, where the members are of one heart and one soul, sharing their deepest convictions as well as their possessions, and having all things common. The wonder and joy of it must be experienced to be believed (TBM, 93).

The Gospel of Jesus Christ is not comfortable to the self-centred man (TBM, 103).

Complete trust about the future *is* a task. I hate uncertainty and not knowing what I can and ought to do. When fear comes in, I "stew" and faith ceases. In the train of that kind of fear, all the old problems of temptation come back. The selfward look is fatal: only the Godward look is full of hope. I am learning that following Christ means taking life day by day, finding strength for the task at hand, and trusting the rest of it—all of it (TBM, 126).

Yet some of the deepest lessons I have learned, of patience, of trust, of the willingness to fail, have come through the surrender of the consequences of my wrong choice to God. . . . God can and will support me. He knows where I can be trusted, and where I am still unfaithful. To Him belongs the plan and its fulfillment. If illness comes, I can through it seek ways to grow;—a special kind of growth. Only no kicking! So long as the barriers of sin—rebellion, self-pity, the sins which fester in idleness—are faced and destroyed through confession, prayer and forgiveness, spiritual growth need never stop. Whatever happens to the body, our souls can live and live indeed, come what may. This is the life that makes us free (TBM, 127).

I thought of . . . the kind of life which the Fellowship called for. That night I decided to "launch out into the deep:" and with the decision to cast my will and my life on God, there came an indescribable sense of relief, of burdens dropping away (TBM, 134).

The great necessity for Christian work today is the forging of an unbreakable human fellowship under God (TBM, 136).

The only work to do is God's will. That is always primary, all-important (TBM, 138).

So long as the life is preoccupied with its own problems, antipathies, moods, it will be bumptious, critical, insensitive, defiant—anything to make up for its conscious inferiorities and maladjustments. But when the releasing honesty of facing its failures and faults has been given, and the worst is known and accepted and then surrendered to God, the whole flavour of living is changed. No longer is one himself the emotional centre of all things, taking everything as personal to himself, but he begins to live most fully in the problems and remaking of other personalities. Here is found a reason and a use for all the suffering through which one has passed: it is to be used in understanding and helping others. Here is a spiritual call and commission which is also a perfect psychological sublimation (TBM, 158).

The effect on [the sensitive soul] was the establishment of such confidence in God that he forgot his ordinary lack of confidence in himself. Thus it is that men come to spiritual maturity (TBM, 160).

Now the problem with [the intellectual man] is not only "moral," in the broad sense; it is also dispositional. He faces not only the common problems of inner conflict which disturb us all, but his very intellectuality may be a wall between him and common men, and it may be also a refuge into which he retreats away from human reality. There is an undertow towards books, in a life like this, which *may* be as destructive of the highest usefulness as a taste for gin, or a temper of laziness (TBM, 177).

For if we truly define sin as "anything that walls us off from God, or from other people," then self-consciousness and discomfort in the presence of sinners and pagans and unbelievers is a real sin, and has got to go as any other sin (TBM, 177–78).

But the spirit and power of this message is essentially a thing to be caught by spiritual fellowship, and by the guidance of the Holy Spirit, and not by imitation or study. I feel a real danger that people will think they understand the movement because they have read about it: nobody understands it until he experiences something of what lies behind the verse in the First Epistle of St. John: "That which we have seen and heard declare we unto you, that ye also may have fellowship with us: and truly our fellowship is with the Father, and with His Son Jesus Christ." The true exegesis of that verse is not found in Bible commentaries, but in a working fellowship of witnessing Christians (TBM, 181–82).

I have seen a good many young ministers establish this kind of real spiritual relationship with someone in their congregation for the first time: and it was as though they felt that *now,* at least, their work had begun. And most often it had been achieved by the willingness of the minister to share his own real self, struggles, sins and all, and to begin, not as a superior or "director," but as an equal,–two honest people in need searching for more of God (TBM, 187).

My life happens to be lived in the midst of spiritual experience. I am one of a growing company of people who believe that the world needs God more than it needs anything else, and who have found a way by which God becomes real. I live in constant touch with people in whose lives spiritual events are taking place (GATY, 3).

Where God guides, He provides (GATY, 136).

People need more than coal and food and a roof: they need faith and courage and love of life and other people. They need more than materials for life, they need direction, values, a working way of life, religion (GATY, 154).

Christianity has been a constant awakening of people to the existence and the worth of other people (GATY, 182).

The root of the malady is estrangement from God—estrangement from Him in people that were made to be His companions. . . . It is extremely hard, and in most cases frankly impossible, for anyone to secure results which are fundamentally spiritual without using any spiritual means, or fulfilling any spiritual conditions (RR, 5–6).

The great contribution of Jesus to the life of the world is not ethical, but personal and spiritual. Father Tyrrel said, "Nothing is original in the righteousness preached by Jesus." One can match many of His ideas in the Old Testament, and even in certain of the ancient Chinese sages. Honor His teachings as you may; they are immensely lofty, but they are not found in Him for the first time. The difference lies in the quality He puts into the old idea, in His uncompromising obedience to it, and, more particularly, in the nature of the relationship with God which He brings to this accepted ethical ideal. What stands out as you ponder the gospels is that He who uttered these sayings is, far beyond them, the important thing. In the gospels you will not come upon a set of wholly new ideas; but you will discover a Personality which transcends all moral ideas, and from whom these high principles pour as sunlight from the sun. Jesus' *person* is the priceless gift of God to men—not His teachings, which are secondary. Principles are meaningless without personal embodiment. Granted Jesus, the teachings follow (RR, 36).

Christianity means only one thing: it means relationship with Christ (RR, 42).

What does it mean to accept Christ? Nothing humiliating, or superstitious, or irrational. You allow Him to set in motion a relationship between you. You enter upon a new companionship. Sherwood Eddy defines a Christian as "one who is living up to all the meanings he finds in Christ." If there are theological problems which hinder, clear them up as you can, remembering always their relatively inferior importance to the "reality of the relation to Christ." Take as much as you can, and work for more. Believe all you can, and don't trouble too much about the rest. Whitwell Wilson says that "some received Him as a prophet, and received the prophet's reward: or as a righteous man, and had the righteous man's reward. He did not denounce these Unitarians. He only made it clear that according to their faith would it be unto them. The limit of blessing was with them, not with Him. They take *part*, where he offers all." Some people must in honesty remain Unitarians until they have an experience of Christ which cannot be interpreted in terms of a merely human Christ. Seek the deeper experience (RR, 43).

The measure of a man's inward Christianity is the depth of his faith in the goodness of God and the sufficiency of Christ. The measure of his outward Christianity is his degree of daring to apply the doctrine of love—the most revolu-

tionary doctrine ever enunciated–in all relationships. The
man of the world plays safe with people, fencing himself
round with fortifications against injury, hatred, loss of prop-
erty or position; the man of Christ freely, foolishly, incred-
ibly trusts people for something better than the best there
is in them, committing himself and his to them without
reserve or suspicion (RR, 50).

The greatest, and in the end perhaps the only permanent,
service one can render to another is to help him on with his
character. Poor human means fall very short in this; if you
doubt this, try it with any person long in the grip of an
engulfing sin. "Influence" is weak and temporary and local
enough at best. The only thing that helps forever is God. . . .
What have you got to give? No man can give away this pre-
cious gift of the religion of Jesus Christ without having at
least the beginnings of it hidden away deep within himself.
In the end it comes back to the same question: *What kind
of a person are you?* Are *you* bound hand and foot with selfishness and sin? Are *your* sympathies shriveled and small?
Can God get through *you* into another life? Religion, if real,
will thrust varying kinds of persons into these forms of direct
and indirect service, according to their gifts (RR, 54–55).

Let's change the world! What do we need? We need a lot
of lesser and contributory things: better houses for some
people to live in, better education, better health, better recreation facilities, better laws. But what we really need is much
more than these, or the sum of them. We need an entirely
new kind of world, where people know how to get on with
each other because they have found the answer to their own
problems, and therefore to the problems of other people,
through substituting the guided plan of God for their own
plans. . . . How change? By being honest . . . about your
lacks, your sins, your want of power. By seeking out people
who have power, and finding out how they got it, and shar-

ing with them your needs. By surrendering yourself to God, with all your sins and faults and limitations. By accepting God's forgiveness and His promise that those who hunger and thirst after what He has, shall be filled. A man came to me in need, not of money or work or health, but of spiritual overhauling. The faith of his childhood had grown cold. He had sought among the cults, and they had left him unsatisfied. He came back to his own church. He shared with me that his problems were resentment, worry, fear and pride. That was definite. We went into the chapel of our church and he gave his problems and himself to God before the altar. A city, a country, a whole generation were represented in that man. When what happened to him happens to enough of us, the world will begin to come right. You know the story about the man whose child was looking for something to do, and the father tore up a map of the world and told the child to put it together again. In a short time the child came back with it all spread outright on a board, and the father asked how he did it so quickly. The child said, "I found on the other side the picture of a man's face, and I put that together first. You see, when you get the man right, the world will take care of itself" (GC, 8–10).

God gives all of us light in proportion to our willingness to have it (GC, 11).

The will and voice of God are the supreme and final authority to be obeyed; but those who are dedicated and experienced know more than the rest of us about human nature, the world we deal with, the way to work, and God's plan, and they deserve the co-operation and loyalty and obedience of the rest of us (GC, 13).

That means to me the inward certainty of being single-minded. It does not mean the certainty of continuous perfection, for none of us has that; but we can have a mind single towards God, which is undiscouraged and undeterred by its own failures, simply because its final refuge and strength are in God, not in self. That gives us a freedom from inferiority, from insincerity, which is convincing to others because we are convinced ourselves. There are people so morally sound, so clàd with spiritual insight, that you know no power of evil can make much headway with them. St. Paul wants us like that (GC, 30).

For me selfishness is considering everything outside myself as it impinges on myself. It can run from hoping nobody will take the best piece of celery on the dish, to the treason of not falling in with a great spiritual plan as guided men and women see it because it interrupts my own plans. It generally has to do with staying in the comfortable rut, and avoiding the inconvenience of listening to a new idea. And I find it terribly, disillusioningly possible to be very selfish about being unselfish, and expecting others to stand aside for my particular kind of unselfish plan. At base, selfishness is sitting still when *we* know that we have got to do the things we want other people to do . . . (GC, 98).

None of us gets across this earth without some pain of body and of mind. Few of us escape some constitutional weakness or defect which causes us limitation, difficulty or shame. . . . Let Him show us how to feel and believe with Him that life is no accident, but an adventure; that suffering is no punishment, but perhaps a reminder, and certainly an opportunity. . . . We are nowhere saying that evil is good: we are saying that the spiritual victory of life is in making evil work toward a good end, and produce in the end a good result. And if that is to happen, there can be no running away from suffering. . . . Very often difficulty and trouble is life nudging us to say that we are taking things the wrong way (GC, 102–104).

Do you know where about nine out of ten of the difficulties which we encounter in our daily life come from? Not from an unkind fate, nor a cruel universe, nor the sins of other people, but from our personal withdrawal from responsibility somewhere in the past, something God handed us to do and we handed it back; and it threw out the course of events and spoiled the plan of God. And, in consequence, we are not *what* we ought to be, and we are not *where* we ought to be. The answer for the problems which many of us face to-day does not lie in any direct solution of them whatever: it lies in the general readiness to take more responsibility for other people, and for this nation. Some of us remain children and inferior children at that, because we do not want to carry fully adult responsibility. God is trying to move us out into a much wider orbit of living, a much greater degree of self-giving, much clearer thinking, much more united action, a truer patriotism, a larger commitment to His kingdom. . . . So, you see, the answer to the special problem or problems of daily living that you face lies in your whole orientation to God (GC, 120).

And I should want to say a particular word about the amazing adequacy of Christ. He is alive, and He is a Person, and He is within reach of you and me. Of the best life that has been lived for twenty centuries, He is the author. The best men and women I know owe everything to Him. He does not save them from the hard knocks that life brings to us all, surely by some design: but He saves them from bitterness, from rebelliousness, from the feeling of destitution and futility. When trouble comes, they do not worry, but rather wait for His full purpose to emerge through the trial. That much I see in others. And what I see for them, that I have experienced for myself. I am not old, and outwardly life has slipped along smoothly and happily for me: but you know that no man can live at all, in his own or others' experience, without inward struggle, battle, temptation, suffering. I can say to you without reserve or quibbling, that Jesus Christ satisfies. He puts a purpose into life it never had before. He shares all its loads and its perplexities. He literally and actually stoops into my life to give me help in the hour of temptation, as often as I let Him come. He makes people happy, not with the hard indifference to trouble of the Stoic, not with the soft indifference of the professional optimist, but with that joy of His own which caused Him to cry out, "Be of good cheer—I have overcome the world" (RTW, 17).

Christ offers us three things. The first is *forgiveness* for the past. He holds out the heart of God as willing to forgive anyone who comes in honest penitence and says he is sorry and means to stop. He makes matters right between us and Him. As a friend said to me this week, "The past is *gone.*"

The second is power to stop sinning. None of us does very well at overcoming sin, but when we do, we know that it has not been all our own doing. Co-operation, yes, but not our own sole effort. For "every virtue we possess, and every victory won, and every thought of holiness, are His alone."

And the third is, the *Cross* to make up for the mass of unatoned, unforgiven, unwashed sin. There is a heap of it. Some I have not recognized. Some I have not had heart to confront and deal with. Some I committed with Christ almost standing by. I can do nothing about it. There is absolutely no excuse for it. I cannot honestly say I tried not to do it. Nothing in me can handle that sin. Only the stooping and infinite mercy of God, taking my sin upon Him, can deal with it, shrive it, obliterate it. The Cross is the only solution. And without it the revelation of God in Christ and the Ideal of man in Christ would leave a terrible incompleteness. Christ alone holds in His hand the key and the cure for sin. Plenty of sages, with ideals to offer. Plenty of good people, with advice. But only one Saviour, to offer a solution for human sin (RTW, 26–27).

A psychiatrist said to me a few weeks ago that ninety percent of the people who came to him needed to have restored their faith in the worthwhileness of living. That is not a material matter, it is profoundly a spiritual matter (RTW, 81).

I dare to say that the profoundest understanding of human beings is impossible except upon a basis of personal acquaintance and sympathy; and that without religion, and the peculiar insight into life which genuine religion brings, the highest kind of sympathy cannot be developed (RTW, 82).

Do not deal with symptoms, but with causes. Get to men's hearts, and change them . . . (RTW, 114).

How many people, as they contemplate the possibility of starting to live the Christian life, want to see the end from the beginning, want to know at the outset just what will be the cost and the outcome. Will this inevitably bring me happiness? May I have to cut my connections with my friends? Would I have to pull out of the business, if I found something shady in its operations? May I hold on to the minor self-indulgence which I love?

Or again, how often they ward off the fundamental issue of deciding for Christ by running up numberless bypaths which lead nowhere. Many a man sits opposite to me in conversation, asking vague questions about Christianity which if they were answered would not alter by a fraction the smallest detail of his life, trifling over irrelevant abstractions while Christ stands in the midst waiting for his choice. And I believe Jesus says to men like that: "I chose a path which began on the bright slopes of Galilee, and closed on a dark hill outside Jerusalem. Shall not the servant tread it still? Leave off your fears for your own future, and your footless questions about interesting spiritual abstractions. What are they to thee? Follow thou Me" (RTW, 114–15).

We do not know the *whole* story of anybody's life but our own: they may need chastening, reminding, softening, testing in ways we know nothing of. We generally can account for the events in our own life, if we wait long enough for God to work through His whole plan. But it is idle to speculate and wonder, where we cannot know all the facts. We may destroy the very faith which would help another to interpret his sorrow helpfully, if we ourselves are unbelieving about it (RTW, 115).

The depth of spiritual life is partly measured by our understanding of the Word of God. Modern Christianity is full of good works, but we are weak on scholarship and on deep Bible study (RTW, 127).

I believe that the primary work of the Church is the remaking of the inner lives of individuals, through the power of the living Christ. . . . You will not find many to dispute you that the greatest need of our time lies in the discovery of some integrating force for human personality (CC, 13).

I am the minister of a New York City parish, and in general I preach once a Sunday. That sermon requires of me between six and twelve hours of work beside the general mulling-over which may go on for years before one preaches the sermon. For twenty-five minutes several hundred people are within the sound of my voice. What comes of it? Our age is in a hurry for a "quick sale," and is apt to lose sight of how much is accomplished by preaching and religious reading, in the gradual enlarging of horizons, the extension of sympathies, and steady upbuilding of moral and spiritual convictions. Yet I often feel that my people's

minds are tired—tired of the sound of words, tired of following an abstract train of thought. I am only sure that the
sermon has struck fire when it brings someone to me in the
porch of the church, asking to talk privately. And when I
sit down with him, I find that the sermon is only a point of
departure, and I must begin all over again and re-translate
its real meaning into the terms of that individual's life. Here
I can begin to convey to him quite a different kind of idea:
namely, stories of living people, people like himself, faced
with just his problems, and therefore pertinent, not to life
in general, but to his particular situation now. This is in the
realm of "news," not "views" (CC, 15).

I believe that we have also made a great mistake to think
that we could set religion forward by mere intellectual
defence of it. If this could be done, the theological colleges
would have converted the world long ago. One pays respects
to the scholars and the teachers who make the historic facts
and truths of Christianity accessible to us: but this alone
never changed anybody. Our modern deference to the intellectual has somehow spread the notion abroad that religion
is primarily a set of ideas, and that a person gets at it by the
dissection of it with his wits. Nothing could be further from
Jesus' thought, or His way with people. He never argued
with anybody. In a personally modest, generally in a con-
ciliatory, sometimes in a frankly dogmatic fashion, He put
before people the truth of His Gospel. It always had theological roots and implications, but the truth was usually put
in the form of pictures and stories. The Church as a whole
needs to learn the truth of Henry Drummond's great words,
that we do not need to prove things to people, but only to
let them see things. The tragic thing is that a person can be
intellectually persuaded of the truth of Christianity without
knowing its power in all the recesses of his life. I do not
know any people who more desperately need a full and
releasing experience of the power of the living Christ than

some of those to whom the ideas of Christianity are both true and familiar. We have succeeded in converting the wits of a good many people to Christ's principles. But one often finds them longing for true spiritual experience and power and inner joy (CC, 21–22).

What does it *mean* to serve any one? Surely nothing less than to aim at his own highest potentiality, the redemption of his personality through the fullest experience that he can have of God. In the process, we may manifest common humanity by such satisfaction of his physical necessities as we can offer: but anyone who has thought with any depth about life knows that the *great* service, the service which exceeds all other services, is the impartation of transforming spiritual experience. What use is all this regimentation of kind people in ranks of human service, without so much as finding out whether those who serve have themselves deeply *been* served, whether those who seem in a position to offer relief are really in such a position because their own lives have been deeply and radically healed by the Spirit of God (CC, 25)?

The Christian life consists in a current of spiritual electricity which runs through three angles of a triangle: God, myself, and other people. A block anywhere in the circuit will put a stop to the current (CC, 49).

The failure of religious workers to take sufficient time to help people to share everything, and their failure to share themselves in equal and humble fellowship, has damned despair and unbelief into more people than the activity of all the atheists. Who ever heard of a doctor who began his cure before he found out what was the matter! Yet hundreds of ministers are dealing in "cure-Christianity," which means the recommendation of solution before one knows the problems. You will never do effective work with individuals unless you have first fully caught their attention and made them want what you have; and unless you have learned the secrets of their lives, and they have told you what kind of people they are underneath where most people do not see them (CC, 79).

There must be a decision in which the will gathers up the facts which the mind has collected, and the aspiration the heart has felt, and packs them into a moral choice. This is the act of self-surrender which is man's part in his own conversion, the step which puts him in position to receive the grace of God which alone converts. For countless thousands of Christians, conversion is an experience at which they look with mystification from a distance. St. Paul was converted, and there was a drunk somewhere in a rescue mission that they have heard about; but such things simply happen in the Providence of God, and for our part we seem to have nothing to do with it. I believe that is not Christian teaching. The "whosoever" of the Gospel means that there is a moral and spiritual prerequisite that any one can fulfill, and having done so, may expect the grace of God to change the life. Surrender is a handle by which an ordinary person may lay hold of the experience of conversion. It is the first step, the step of the will. In order to make surrender the decision of the whole life, and not merely the emotion of moment, it needs to be filled with practical content: we must help people to see just what they are surrendering to God, their fears, their sins, most of all their *wills*, putting God's will once and for all ahead of every other thing. When these items are cleared through talking and sharing, they can be lumped together, and with the self flung out in abandon upon the mercy and the power of God (CC, 79–80).

Living religion is likely to begin in an individualistic experience. Through the help of another, or alone, we first discover the inner world of the Spirit, and its tremendous power in regulating and enhancing ordinary life.

Then as time goes on, we grow reflective about our experience. We find that others have been in the same places and known the same truths. By comparison and contrast we correct and enrich our own experience through historic perspective. We come to see the validity of much that we once thought was purely formal. We come to attach more and more importance to those eternal and absolute verities of the Christian religion, which are not dependent upon our own fluctuating and uncertain moods. We become interested in theology, almost in spite of ourselves: because most of us are intellectually curious, and want at least to be intellectually honest. Theology is only the attempt to think systematically about the things man believes and discovers about God (IIBL, 7).

Trouble always turns us in, or turns us out. We either feel sorry for ourselves, or we feel sorry for all the rest of mankind. Trouble is a kind of sacrament: and God means it to work a work of grace in us, and then to open our hearts to all human needs. You have heard this before, and there is nothing new in it: but maybe the *experience* would be new if it came and transfigured your trouble into sympathy (IIBL, 44).

It is not fullness of years, or mere quantitative achievement which marks a complete life. It is a quality of perfectness in the life itself. Many have done more and lived more whose lives were never complete. Completeness is really a matter of inner wealth and peace. It is a quality of self-sufficiency in the presence of the bafflements and perplexities and sufferings of life, or rather a matter of God-sufficiency (IIBL, 106–107).

You say to me, How can one person "bear" the sins of another? Let me tell you a story. Some weeks ago a friend of mine who is a minister of Christ had a man come to him in desperate spiritual need. Like most of those who are in great spiritual need, he was also in great temporal and financial need as well. The minister asked him to stay at his house. But the man's pride was too great for that, he said—he had at least always made his own way. Now the chief thing that was the matter with that man was not the sin of his body, but the sin of his mind; not his lust and his drunkenness, but his pride. Before he could be rid of his gross sins, something must break down his pride. There was no way to break it down except to make him *accept something he didn't deserve, to give him something which it was literally impossible for him to pay for.* He finally consented to come: and with his pride down, he was in position to accept something else than hospitality from the minister, and he found Christ through him. The minister paid both the board-bill and the cost of giving that man hours of time to redeem him. The man gave nothing and received twice: the minister got nothing and gave twice. But the process of redemption began at the moment when the man *accepted something which he knew he did not deserve, and was given something which it was literally impossible for him to pay for.* That is what I call "bearing" another person's sins. And that is the precise and definite aim of the Cross of Christ: to destroy our pride by persuading us to accept a gift which we do not deserve, by giving us something which we could not possibly pay for. There is no more subtle or dangerous pride in the world than the pride of being righteous without God's help. The indispensability of the Cross lies here: that the man whose righteousness comes up out of himself is bound to be self-righteous,—and self-righteousness is worse than no righteousness at all. We can only be really good by derivation. We can only really be good by being given something to be thankful for. The man, therefore, who knows beyond doubt that he has been saved through the atoning death of Jesus Christ has no place left in his life for pride—all he has is abashed and astonished thankfulness. The Cross is a frontal attack of God upon man's pride. Its first and chief message is, "You cannot save yourself!" Salvation comes through the mercy of God, not through the merit of man.

But the Cross does something else beside crushing the pride out of us. It restores us as the conscious children of God's love. Its final word is not concerned with how little we *can do* for ourselves, but with how much God *has done* for us. It ought to make us think of the cost of our salvation to God: but the heart of it is, "Never mind the price—it has been paid" (IIBL, 113–15).

The very beginning of our religion is nothing we do, it is something done for us—a gift to us. Grace comes first, then character. Salvation first, then service (IIBL, 135).

Remember that life has a purpose, which is the development of human character through struggle and moral discrimination. . . . (IIBL, 140).

The heart of Christianity is relationship with God, not ethics—they follow. The pride of thinking that we can make ourselves worthy in God's sight is as great a sin as the pride of thinking that we may ignore God altogether. The deepest thing in the Christian religion is not anything that we can do for God, it is what God has already done for us (IIBL, 161).

Many of us are wrong with God and wrong with each other: and what we need is to be right with God, and right with each other. Towards God we need repentance, and towards man we need restitution. The first step is not resurrection, it is crucifixion. . . . It is the crucifixion of pride, narrowness, stupidity, ignorant prejudice, intolerance, fixed viewpoints about other people, laziness, lack of vision, self-satisfaction, conventionality that we need. There is no resurrection without crucifixion. The reason Christ's Cross is so central is that there is a cross at the center of life anyway: either God's will is crucified on it so that our will may prevail; or our will is crucified on it so that God's will may prevail (NA, 5).

One of her boys felt tremendously the lack of God in his life, but never till that week had found anybody he could talk with about it, or find the way out. That week seven people in that one family had begun actually to put God first in their lives. One let go of fear and long-standing resentment. One let go of inferiority and withdrawal right in the family. Another let go of drugs. Walls came down in a frankness of understanding which they had believed impossible (NA, 7).

Don't we need to go back to Christ, and see whether we have lost something? So far as I can remember He said almost nothing about character: but He did say once to a very good citizen that what he needed was to be born again. Some people would understand that better if you said "he needed to be *changed.*" Suppose we began in this day to say that our great need was for "changed lives," and then gave the world the example of a changed life in creative dynamic, instead of stodgy conservatism—what do you think might be the effect? It is my own profound belief that changed lives are the Christian answer for moral character (NA, 16).

If you live by the say-so of the opinions of others, you will end up trying to live by their experiences—and you can't do that (NA, 26).

All of us seek security in some form, because we need it and must have it. Physical life goes out when we do not have a minimum of food, clothes and shelter. And none of us can live without human interdependencies and attachments, both economic and personal: we can neither provide ourselves with the necessities of life without the help of other people nor do most of us want to live without their society. That applies to the highest life imaginable on earth. It applies to Christ. He lived in a material world, where He had to eat and sleep and protect Himself from the swiftly changing climate in which He lived. He could have had no social joy in life, nor could He have accomplished and continued His work, without the company and help of other people or without very real dependence upon them. But no one could say that His ultimate dependence was on the material world or on other people within it. His ultimate security was in God. And we must honestly ask ourselves where lies our final security: whether it lies in people and things or whether it lies in God (NA, 35).

And we must not forget those who put their security in false religion. Many people turn to God when they are in trouble, and that is as good a time to turn to Him as any other: there is nothing cowardly or unsporting about recognizing under any circumstances that you've been trying to live in God's world without God, and admitting to Him that you were wrong, and are suffering the consequences of being wrong, and want to come back to Him again repentant, and begin to live with Him as the recognized Source of life and achievement and happiness. But if you come to religion seeking health and wealth and happiness, instead of seeking God and His plan for you and His will for the world, you can find the promise of these things only in a spurious religion which has lost authentic touch with Christianity (NA, 38–39).

And as people's faith in one after another solution rises and falls, one feels a deepening discouragement. The need for a real answer grows daily greater. I believe that it lies in an altered human nature. And I believe that there is no deep and permanent alteration in human nature until we find God and His power in our lives to direct us. It looks to me as though this world was constructed to run on the power of faith in God and love towards one another. When we try to run it on faith in ourselves and self-interest, it is like trying to run on water a car that was built to run on gasoline. When it won't run, it doesn't mean that there is anything organically the matter with the car, it just means that it won't function without the right kind of power. The fact may be, not that the world is unfit to live in, as a lot of pessimists and skeptics would tell us, but that we are unfit to live in it. If we were different, the world might be different. A lot of us look out almost hopelessly on a world like this, and say, What can I do today? What impression can one unit like myself make upon the mass of confusion and strife about me today? The answer is that we can be different. And we can begin to help other people to be different. And out of a few really different people in the right places we can begin building a new society on the ashes of the old (NA, 70).

[We] found what we all find, that it is not nearly so difficult to get people to undertake the spiritual pilgrimage as it is to get them to keep on with it through the bewilderments and moods and misgivings of its early stages, till they come finally to the place where the promises are fulfilled (NA, 90).

One must in honesty reject faith entirely, or one must find a reasonable way to maintain it (CF, 96).

People are more important than things: He may want to touch somebody spiritually through you by means of a business contact. I know a magnificent trained-nurse. She is quick, ready, intelligent, sympathetic. She is also a devoted

Christian. I asked her if she used her faith and got it across to her patients. She said they were not allowed to talk religion unless asked about it. I said, "Can't you make them ask?" "How?" she asked. "By living it twenty-four hours a day and manifesting the power and joy you have till they are dying of curiosity about it." She said often patients asked her what kept her so spruce and cheerful. Now she would tell them. It is the extra creative mile in life's ordinary occupations, which fills them with real joy and real fruitfulness (CF, 160).

11

How to Know
the Will of God

Not every one that saith unto me, Lord, Lord,
shall enter into the kingdom of heaven; but he that
doeth the will of my Father which is in heaven.
Matthew 7:21

If any man will do his will, he shall know of the
doctrine, whether it be of God, or whether I speak
of myself.
John 7:17

Speak, LORD; for thy servant heareth.
1 Samuel 3:9

Lord, what wilt thou have me to do?
Acts 9:6

Shoemaker frequently wrote concerning the need for
and the method of learning the will of God. Early on, he
wrote the following chapter in *Religion That Works,* using
Henry Drummond's views as a starting point. Shoemaker

often wrote that God's general or universal will is to be found in the Bible. He believed that if a person is willing to obey and act on the universal will of God, as set forth in Scripture, God will disclose to him God's particular will—if he listens. Prayer is the beginning and the end of knowing God's will—first there must be surrender to His will, then openness to His plan, and lastly a request that He make His will known.

Now, anyone who knows much about people spiritually comes to feel, sooner or later, that the greatest problem any of us face is the problem of what we shall do about the will of God. When we come to believe in God at all, we come to believe in Him as having something definite to say about our lives. To believe in the fact of the will of God is only to believe in God in the concrete. As you cannot pray without words, so you cannot imagine God apart from His desires which touch us. There is at the heart of religion this marriage between the mystical and the moral. And Henry Drummond, with inerrant insight, went often into this great problem. It was the love of his life to do the will of God. He was no glib and facile interpreter of what it was: he spent long hours searching his Bible for light on the question. And when he had finished his study, this scholar seeking a truth of metaphysics, this devoted Christian trying to know the heart and mind of his God, he wrote down in the fly-leaf of his Bible these eight points:

1. Pray.
2. Think.
3. Talk to wise people, but do not regard their decision as final.
4. Beware of the bias of your own will, but do not be too much afraid of it (God never unnecessarily thwarts a man's nature and likings, and it is a mistake to think that His will is in the line of the disagreeable).

5. Meantime, do the next thing, for doing God's will in small things is the best preparation for knowing it in great things.
6. When decision and action are necessary, go ahead.
7. Never reconsider your decision when it is finally acted upon; and—
8. You will probably not find out till afterwards, perhaps long afterwards, that you were led at all.

Now, let me take these steps one at a time, and embroider them a little in detail, reminding you first that I am not sure I have in everything caught the sense of Henry Drummond, and that I am packing my own meaning into his phrases.

1. "Pray." It is a common thing to run to God in petulant and frantic demand, asking Him to tell us what to do. This may be the sudden reversal of a life of self-seeking and self-guidance; and it is not to be wondered at if not much guidance comes from Him. What we often seek is His approval, not His will. When we come in a great honesty, having put our own wills behind us, seeking candidly the mind of the Lord, it is generally rather plain sailing: a mood or disposition comes upon us with light in it, or a direct thought flits across our mind with illumination. These experiences are too common amongst Christians for any of you to pooh-pooh them until you have tried honestly. But when we come only in curiosity, merely wondering what God might like us to do, quite different is the result. We get nowhere, prayer is a fog, we get up anxious and fretful and in a stew. To find God's will in prayer demands a colossal honesty in our minds. A man recently disputed my use of the word honesty in this connection: he said willingness and unselfishness I might use, but honesty implied dishonesty in coming to God with our minds made up. Yet this is precisely what we are; we are dishonest when we prejudice the will of God by trying to twist it into our own will: we are not honest

with facts, especially the great fact that God's plan may not be our plan. "My thoughts are not your thoughts" is true more often than we care to remember. So that to pray for God's will to be revealed we must be ready and willing to have it revealed, and come to Him with an open mind.

Yet I recall a friend of mine speaking of his desire to know what he ought to do with his life. I asked if he had prayed about it. He said that he had, and he asked God what to do: but that if God had said certain things, he would not have been willing to do them. That is not prayer: it is a kind of blasphemy instead. It points the truth that no man can see the will of God who is not willing to see it. One of Drummond's favourite verses in this connection was John 7:17: "If any man *willeth* to do his will, he shall know." And wrapped up in that little verse there lies more empirical spiritual experience than almost anywhere else I know. This, then, is the first guide—to pray.

2. "Think." There is a moral obligation to be as intelligent as you can. Turn over the possibilities in your mind. Face all the facts you can find, honestly and fearlessly. I am not afraid of too much thought in religion, I am only afraid of too little of it. It is not sound reasoning which steals men's religion, it is half-baked rationalizing. Some people use their brains to convince themselves they ought to do what they want to do. Jesus says, against this kind of thing: "Judge not according to appearance, but judge righteous judgment." It may be a good thing to put down the pros and cons in two written columns, and weigh one against the other. If the decision concerns your life-work, face the needs of the world frankly, as well as your own qualifications. We are apt to be too subjective in some of these questions. I believe we do well to look out on the world, and ask what it is which that world needs most, and then ask ourselves how we can best supply that need—rather than to turn in upon ourselves and ask what riches and talents lie hidden within us which we must find a way to turn loose upon the world. Look out,

and assemble all the facts you can. There is nothing the matter with using human brains, so long as an honest character lies behind them. But this is an age of more self-deception, under the guise of intellectual honesty, than any I know about. Remember that, when all is said and done, God may communicate His wish to you, and knock your thinking endwise. To be thoroughgoingly, intellectually honest, you will consider as the greatest factor of all the will of God.

3. "Talk to wise people, but do not regard their decision as final." That is, don't expect them to make up your mind for you. Consult them for what they are worth. But make the decision your own. There are always a lot of people in the world who like to talk to ministers, as if we knew it all: they run to us to settle things they ought to be close enough to God to settle for themselves. And we are always in danger of priding ourselves upon our influence, and handing out packages of advice, when as a matter of fact we ought to be dealing with a larger issue, the issue of their surrender to God's will, and their own search for what it is. Now, don't discuss this with just anybody you happen to think about, but with people who love God and His will and are themselves putting the kingdom of heaven first.

Go to really wise people, wise with God's wisdom: and He will often speak to you through them, as generally He does speak through others. But let this talk be for a *clearing* of the issue, not for a *settlement* of it. What they say to you is valid only insofar as it rings a bell in your own heart.

4. "Beware of the bias of your own will, but do not be too much afraid of it (God never unnecessarily thwarts a man's nature and likings, and it is a mistake to think that His will is in the line of the disagreeable)." Drummond was talking to Scotsmen with consciences a yard long when he added to his universal warning: "Beware of the bias of your own will," the balance, "But do not be too much afraid of it." I think the first half of it is probably more applicable to us. We are not likely to err on the side of interpreting God's

will hardly, but softly. When you consult God and your mind is already partially made up, you need very seriously to beware of that bias, for it will throw out all the calculations. Left to ourselves, we are very likely to please ourselves.

And yet we need the postscript, too: "Do not be too much afraid of it. God never unnecessarily thwarts a man's nature and likings, and it is a mistake to think that His will is in the line of the disagreeable." It is a mistake, and a great one. I heard a woman say within a week that whatever was the hardest thing to do was probably God's will: but I do not believe that. Some people think God goes around hunting up hard and unhappy jobs, and then trailing them down and loading the jobs off on them. To make God that kind of a supernatural taskmaster is to be unchristian in our thought of Him. There are hard jobs to be done, and somebody has got to do them. But I feel sure that God made us for a particular piece of work, and that we shall never be fully happy until we find that work. You may not think it looks like you would enjoy it: but if it is His place you will, and you will never really be happy anywhere else.

5. "Meantime, do the next thing, for doing God's will in small things is the best preparation for knowing it in great things." Some are so preoccupied with the obvious that they never get above it to take a look at the whole: but some also are so busy with the abstract they never see the concrete, nor complete the ordinary duty which stares them in the face. A man who is honestly living up to the light he has, to-day, will have more light to-morrow, when he needs it. Sometimes God makes us wait for the full emergence of His plan. If we have been faithful in a few things, He will make us master of many things, revealing as much truth as we can live up to. I know a man in business in downtown New York. He has been soundly changed in his own life, and he loves to bring Christ into the lives of men. He does not know whether God wants him to go into the ministry or not.

Meanwhile he is doing a fine job in an insurance office, and working there until or unless he is guided to go elsewhere. There is an enormous amount of common sense about real religion which we miss sometimes because it is not exactly the common sense of the world at large.

6. "When decision and action are necessary, go ahead." Go ahead fearlessly. God will give you for each step as much light as you really need, and perhaps no more. You may see from here to the next corner, and there the path seems to turn down into the dark. Go that far, and more light will come. Do not wait till you see light on all the road before you: most of us never do see it. The Greeks used to wear lanterns on their shoes: it would throw light about three feet ahead of them, and then they had to take one more step to get three feet more of light. So it is with finding the will of God. You may not see all the sides of a question of importance, yet you must decide it. God will give you *enough* light. Do not rush Him, or the situation; but when you must, let the hammer fall, act on all the light you have, and you will make no mistake. The more you trust God in critical situations, the more you will learn that you can trust Him: and that if you will throw the onus of decision off yourself and on to Him, giving Him only a ready and obedient will, you will be amazed at the way things work out for you.

7. "Never reconsider the decision when it is finally acted upon." That is of immense importance. Every thoughtful person, every conscientious person, wonders again and again about an old decision; wants to go back and tear it up by the roots and ask again why it was ever made. Some people do that about marriage, many do it about their life's work. They acted in all good faith at the time: but later they question their own decision. It is a fatal thing to do. Now, if the decision was made selfishly, we may have to make the best of a bad margin; remembering that God has always a substitute will which goes into the game when the first-string

will is put out. But if they acted under God so far as they understood, it was the best they could do. If trial and difficulty has come since, that was meant to have its place. We should spend our lives on regrets, and many do so spend them, if we spent much time reconsidering decisions that have been already acted upon. *Until* a decision is acted upon, reconsider as much as you like. But afterwards, go forward and banish fear.

8. "You will probably not find out till afterwards, perhaps long afterwards, that you were led at all." I should not put so much of an interval as Drummond implies; for I believe that we often know we acted rightly by a very quick sense of being right, and sometimes by the manifest outworking of God's plan which shows itself quickly. And yet there is an immense truth here. He is talking about totals and broad outlines. And one finds that the great compensation for the steady fleeing-away of the years is a larger and longer look at one's own life, and a clearer view of the path by which he has come. One sees here just the right person coming across one's path to point a truth, or to enlarge a horizon. There we came across that great book that turned us upward. In another place a great sorrow made us tender and kinder. And the map of the will of God is not the track of a railway stretching away before us, but rather the wake of a ship lying white behind us. We see best how clear that path is as we look back upon it over a long period of time. I ask you to-day to look back across your own life—not somebody's else, for we never know all the factors anywhere but in our own—look at your own life, and see whether, if you have acted according to your best, and interpreted events with a will to find God's purpose, things have not marvelously worked together for good.

But we end where we began. Prayer is the heart of the discovery of the will of God. I will defend it against all comers that something happens when a man lays his life open before God, and asks Him to make known His will, which cannot happen by any amount of uninspired thought or human direction. We see into the heart of things in prayer like that. But that kind of prayer is impossible without radical and basic surrender to the will of God first. "If any man willeth to do his will"—this means, no grudging concession to God, but whole-hearted allegiance and the co-operation of one's whole self—"he shall know." The man who knows God's will is the man who loves it. The man who finds out what God wants is the man who cares what God wants, who feels upon him the same kind of burdens God feels and carries. If God can count on you, He can commit His secrets to you. We have got to get on God's side before it's any use to ask what is God's plan.

As Drummond finished his address in Appleton Chapel, at Harvard, thirty-five years ago, he said: "Above all things, do not touch Christianity unless you are willing to seek the kingdom of God first. I promise you a miserable existence if you seek it second." That is true. And the matter with many who call themselves Christians, and have never found any thrill and power in their religion, lies just there: they are not seeking the kingdom first.

But when you do come out on that side with all your heart, and seek the kingdom first, I can promise you not a miserable existence, but the only thing that satisfies on this side of eternity. I say to you that it will be the tragedy of your life to miss the will of God, and the standing and crowning success of your life to find it. There is no other success than to do what God wants you to do.

"Not every one that saith unto me, Lord, Lord, shall enter into the kingdom of heaven; but he that doeth the will of my Father who is in heaven."

God give us the grace to ask: "Lord, what wilt thou have me to do?"

Let us pray:

O God, who in Thy love for us dost plan for us a way far better than our own: Grant us to desire Thy will above all things, and desiring it, to seek it; and seeking it, to find it; and finding it, to serve Thee faithfully and to make Thee known to men. Through Jesus Christ our Lord (RTW, 55–65).

12

Shoemaker Touches the Life of an Alcoholic

Bill Wilson, A.A.'s co-founder, apparently never wrote of or told the details as to how Rev. Sam Shoemaker passed on to him the ideas which Wilson said formed most of the basis for A.A.'s Twelve Steps. Nor did Wilson explain how Shoemaker might have worked with him personally in the early stages of Bill's sobriety. However, Charles Clapp, Jr., who worked personally with Bill's friend, Shep Cornell, and with Shoemaker, and who recovered from alcoholism in the Oxford Group, wrote a book telling his story. Clapp got sober with Shoemaker's help about the same time as Wilson got sober. Clapp's story and his description of his surrender prayer rather closely resemble some of the details in Bill's story—contained in the first chapter of A.A.'s Big Book. Were Clapp's experiences with Shoemaker similar to those of Bill? We do not know, but here are excerpts from *The Big Bender*.[1]

Toward the end of March Samuel M. Shoemaker, rector of Calvary Episcopal Church in New York, returned from a trip to California. I looked forward to meeting this man, for I had heard and read considerable about him. He was one of the leaders of the Group; his church was the center of the Group's activities in the city; it was in Calvary's parish hall that I had attended many meetings.

Sam, as most people called him, was a charming, well-educated man, who looked and acted more like a broker than a minister. Now, I have seen many ministers who try very hard to look like one of the boys, but they always look just like ministers trying to be one of the boys. Sam was different; he was just a damn nice fellow who wasn't acting, wasn't trying to act, and wasn't pretending to be anything but himself.

After listening to him in many meetings, and after having chatted with him a few times, I decided I must either fish, cut bait, or row ashore, in so far as the Group was concerned. This business of trying to ferret out facts had me thoroughly upset. I sought a conference with Sam, feeling that it was the interview to end interviews. I had a lot of questions I wanted to ask and felt confident that when I had heard the answers I would withdraw from Group activity.

I was certain that this business of trying to live on the four Absolutes would not be to my liking; this was especially true of the type of life I was now planning for myself as a bachelor. I made an appointment to meet him at his apartment one afternoon. But just so I would not become too involved with the spiritual, and completely forget myself in a wave of evangelistic salesmanship, I arranged a dinner date with a girl. Believe me, I was taking no chances of doing something rash.

Sam and I talked for three hours. We discussed every angle of the Group and what it stood for, as well as some theology, psychology, sexology, pathology, horse-racing, etc.

His main topic of conversation that day, however, was himself. Frankly and honestly, he told me of his own failures and defeats, what he had done about them, relating them to some of the things I told him of myself. He spoke of his first meeting with Frank Buchman, of the quality of life he saw in that man and how Buchman had shown him the way to turn defeat into victory.

Never before had a man been so frank and honest with me. But—I was not sure that there was a God. "Well," Sam said, "why not try to find out?" "Possibly, at some later time," I replied. I did not want to start anything with that dinner date waiting for me. I felt there would be plenty of time for me to go in for this sort of life. After I reached fifty, then I would not mind slowing up a bit.

When we got to the subject of drinking, I, in true drunkard form, said liquor was no real problem; I could stop at any time; I was at the moment on the wagon, and although liquor had no doubt caused some of my troubles, so had a lot of other things; I drank only to be sociable (I blush to think how many times I have told this lie), and, furthermore, I would probably not drink again for some little time, and then only on special occasions.

Seven o'clock approached, the hour of my date, and I started to take my leave. Sam asked me if I did not want to have a little prayer with him to ask God to reveal Himself to me and show me what He wanted me to do with my life. I said, "Nothing doing—not tonight." Thanking him for being so generous with his time and telling him I would still come to some of the Group meetings, I departed, girlward.

Leaning back in the taxi, I lit a cigarette and, inhaling deeply, thought: Phew! it's a wonder I didn't make an ass of myself and surrender my life or some such fool thing. Then where would I be? No more fun—just a goody-goody. I couldn't stand that. Why, hadn't I just freed myself of having to report home all the time? It had been a nuisance to arrange with the Yale Club to make all those calls. . . . Now tonight, on my old arrangement, I would have felt hampered. . . . It was great to be your own boss . . . and I might have spoiled it all. Sam was very convincing . . . nicer than any minister I had ever known . . . none of that holier-than-thou stuff. . . . Most of them gave me a pain in the. . . . I might go to a meeting occasionally, but not so often . . . too many meetings–that was the trouble. . . . Why, they were actually beginning to mean something to me . . . that would never do. . . . The first thing I knew I would be all sewed up and then what? . . . Lucky I had this date. . . . After I had been with her a while I would get all this rubbish out of my mind . . . yes, that was it–get my mind cleared up . . . this stuff was getting a bad hold on me. . . .

Suddenly the street lights grew dim, the most overwhelmingly powerful feeling gripped me, something inside me said, "You must surrender your life to Me!" Gradually the lights returned to their natural brightness, the gripping feeling left, and I was sitting bolt upright, tingling all over. . . . Soon, the taxi drew up to the curb (Chap. 14, 120–24).

In the restaurant, the lady of the evening and I were shown a table by the head waiter. I felt exactly as though I were walking on air, sure of myself, yet quite puzzled as to what I should do next. As dinner came on, I told her I might have to leave immediately afterward; I would know more after I had made a phone call; it would take me only a moment. . . .

"No. Mr. Shoemaker has gone out for the evening. No one here knows his whereabouts."

In desperation, I phoned Shep Cornell. "Do you know where I can find Sam?"

"Weren't you with him this afternoon?" he asked.

"Yes, but I must find him immediately," I persisted.

"Have you been drinking?" queried Shep, and to my negative reply, "Well, come up to the apartment; I think I know where he is spending the evening."

Returning to the table, I looked straight into the eyes of the girl and asked myself if I really wanted to find Sam or preferred to stay with this most enchanting morsel. As soon as we had dined, I took her to her apartment and hurried off to meet Cornell.

The door of the Cornell apartment opened and Shep looked at me as though he expected me to fall on my face. "Come in," he said. "Why, you aren't drunk, are you?"

"Naturally I'm not," I replied. "Have you found Shoemaker?"

"Yes. He will meet you back at 61 Gramercy Park in half an hour. What is this all about? You act as though you had suddenly gone nuts!"

"I'll tell you some other time. I want to have a talk with Sam before I say anything. I'll just get there in time if I leave now." Sam led me to his study on the second floor. I immediately told him the whole story—a trifle gingerly, fearing he would think I had lost my mind. He listened attentively to the end, then opened up his Bible and read me the story of Paul on the road to Damascus. My eyes nearly popped out of my head. It was the first time I had ever seen any similarity between an incident in the Bible and something that could take place in the world of today. To me, the Bible had always been a vague book, full of "begats" and a lot of other queer words wholly unrelated to modern life. For some little time we talked, Sam telling me of other similar experiences, of startling things in his own life, of the different ways God had of revealing Himself to people. At last we got down on our knees. I prayed out loud for the first time in my life, simply asking God to take my life and run it; I also thanked Him for revealing Himself to me, after I had so definitely turned my back on Him. When I stood up, I felt as though a tremendous weight had been lifted from the back of my neck—as though a veil had been swept away from my eyes . . . and strangely near to strange tears (Chap. 15, 125–28).

For several days I fairly glowed all over and felt as though I were floating around. The nearest similar sort of feeling I had ever experienced was after drinking an "earthquake." This was a cocktail some of us used as a pickup; it consisted of a third each of gin, Scotch, and absinth. I now had all the elated sensation without the guilty tag. There was some confusion in my mind about what I should do next, but I thought this would shortly clear up. I secretly cherished a feeling of having found something that others around me did not know about. It was a jubilant, superior feeling, which at times I wished no one else to be a part of; at other times I wanted to share it with everyone I met. In so far as I was concerned, there was no longer any doubt of the existence of God and I wondered a little if I had not been picked out as His special messenger to this earth (Chap. 16, 129–30).

... during the next two years I was either extremely pious or extremely drunk.

There were times when I came running to the Group and felt very much a part of it. Most of the time, however, I avoided the other members, considering them narrow-minded and dull. On occasions, my denunciation of them was stronger than can be written. Somehow, I never felt I got entirely away from God, for my experience of the taxi was always very real to me. There were times when I wished that I had never known it, since it had produced my conscience. I prayed regularly, except when I was too drunk to do so. I practically demanded that God do this or that for me; or (and this was nearly always in my prayers) I asked God to handle my drinking so that it would not be a problem—in other words, I asked Him to help me drink like a gentleman (Chap. 18, 145–46).

It was not long before I was again on a bender of three days' duration. The third loop occurred in early October and I landed in town before it had ended. There, a former drunk who had completely given up drinking after coming in touch with the Group, cornered me. We spent several hours together and I honestly faced not only the problem of liquor itself, but all the things underneath and back of it all, which had caused me to drink. For the first time, I admitted drinking had me licked; when I drank I lost control of myself and I was the most selfish human being on earth. I definitely determined to turn my life over to God, to try and straighten out all the messes I had caused and to pay whatever price was necessary to get my life, as nearly as I could, on a basis of Absolute Honesty, Purity, Unselfishness, and Love. Since that day in October, 1935, I have not had a drink (Chap. 19, 152).

Life took on an entirely new aspect. When I had made my original beginning, it was as though the first rays of dawn had broken through the darkness of night—now it was the full sunrise in all its glory. That may sound very damn poetic; well, it was! The desire to drink, as well as that indescribable liquor-consciousness, left me immediately. I knew it, but of course no one else could know it, or would believe it. In former times, when I had gone on the wagon and no one took it seriously, I got very irritated. Now it did not even annoy me.

The really setting right of my affairs was a huge job, hasn't been completed yet, and may take years to accomplish—particularly in relation to my debts. It took years to get myself and my affairs into a mess. Therefore, it will take some time to clean up everything. The speed of cleaning up is only retarded by myself; God can work just as fast as I permit.

One of my first steps was to talk over my life completely with some one, and this necessitated going back to Sam Shoemaker, admitting I had not been absolutely honest when I first talked to him. This was hard to do; it made me feel like a perfect stinker to have seen him rather frequently for over two years, yet not to have been completely on the level with him.

There were people I had to see and to whom I had to make restitution. To some I had to write. Only one wrote back a scathing answer, which, strangely enough, did not make me mad or resentful, although I had not become a "turn the other cheek" fellow yet. There still remain many people and situations which pop up or I remember for the first time. These I must see or straighten out in whatever way seems right. This will probably go on for years, as I see new implications to this way of life and see wrongs I attributed to others which definitely belong to me.

Against many Group people I had held resentment. These had to be seen and told exactly how I had felt toward them. At one meeting, composed of some four or five hundred Group people, I told what a "fringer" I had been, but said I was now open to any checking by anyone who saw me going off at a tangent in my former way.

The new life commenced. True, the price was high, but it was worth it. Starting each day by asking God what He wanted me to do, really trying to find His plan; not asking God how to accomplish *my* plan and for Him to show me the easy way; not asking what customers to show to which place, or how to make more money or how to drink properly; but seeking His daily plan, whether it involved standing in the bread line or financial success; not demanding that my needs be met, but leaving to Him what those needs were and following His instructions as to how to take care of them. This works, but not in the way you might imagine.

The first time I considered the idea of God guiding anyone, it all seemed wholly impossible. Surely He would not be interested in the small things in my life, even if He might be concerned in a few major decisions. I believed some general might receive direction from God at the critical point of a battle, the result of which would affect millions of people; or a bishop probably would receive a little help in sending out a proclamation to thousands of human beings; but for me to hear God speak, I felt was really far-fetched, if not ridiculous.

When I eventually reached the point of considering what God would guide one to do, I concluded it would be something very wild, weird, and spectacular. I believed there would probably be a loud ringing of bells, bright lights would shine, a thundering voice would issue some such mysterious instructions as "You should take a certain street car to a definite place, get off, walk two blocks and there you will find a man with a long, red beard."

My first conscious experience of receiving guidance I have mentioned before. This was very dramatic and real. For over two years after this occurred, I was so mixed up by my own selfish desires and plans, it was difficult for me to see clearly and understand God's plan for me. When I cleaned away the debris in my life, I began to understand His plan day by day and to know He really was guiding me. In other words, it had been as though someone were trying to use a radio set which lacked tubes and was in filthy condition.

One way to test quickly a thought or plan is to see if it conflicts with any one of the four standards—Absolute Honesty, Absolute Purity, Absolute Unselfishness, and Absolute Love. It is a certainty God is not going to tell me to do anything which will violate any of these. Should a thought or plan of great moment, or one about which there was some doubt come to me, I check it with others who are living on this basis. Checking is done by talking it all over, clearly and honestly, praying about it, and seeing whether it seems right.

My wife and I start each day with what we call a "quiet time." First, we read something from the Bible or from some book containing Biblical quotations; next we pray, asking God to show us what He wants us to change in ourselves and what He wants us to do that day. Then we listen, writing down whatever comes into our minds.

The idea of a "quiet time" sounded completely screwy to me when I first heard of it. A whole lot of wild, crazy things do not come into my head, as I had expected. The plans for the day unfold themselves with the greatest simplicity; see this person; write the letter I should have written yesterday; pay that bill; it was selfish of me to have done so and so; have the Blanks for dinner; order coal for the furnace; tell my daughter I was sorry I got mad when she did this or that; and so on. The day is planned with adequate time for everything, but believe me, I am busy. On this basis, God certainly does not expect me to sit around and wait for manna to fall from heaven. He expects me to go full steam ahead, using all the brains, pep, power, ingenuity, personality and brawn He has given me and to use them to the maximum.

What adventure! What romance! When I get up in the morning I never know what I am to do. Sometimes it is the usual, but many times it comes to me to call up or see some one I have no apparent reason for calling or seeing. What startling things happen! Countless chances to help others! Some small, trifling things, which lead to gigantic ones.

Should we get into an argument, as husbands and wives often do, we settle our disputes by taking them to God and seeking His answer, His solution. His replies have surprised me no end. At times I have been certain I knew what would come to me, if I sought guidance. Often, yes; usually, it has been very different.

Since I have been trying to live in this way, I have had numerous startling pieces of guidance. Time and again I have felt definitely I should do a certain thing which, reasoned out on a human basis, was absolutely contrary to the usual or accepted practice, and yet, when followed out, caused the most amazing results; some in connection with the home, some with business, and some with friends.

I have discovered God is at all times ready and willing to guide me. When His guidance does not seem to be clear, I find it's because I have let "self" creep in and have clogged up the "wires"; but when they are clear once again, He can talk to me. This statement of some one in the Group is certainly true: "When man listens, God speaks."

Shortly after my initial start in the Group, I did considerable talking about it, usually when I was away from any friends. I did speak at one meeting in Westport which caused a headline in the local paper. Now, instead of yelling about it, I really commenced to live it. As a result, more people came to me to find the solution to their own problems or to find out what to do about some one close to them. "Bill—you know he is drinking terribly and so on," or, "He's so selfish, he won't do this or that." They would predicate this by saying they had seen such a change in me and wanted to know how it happened.

There were some who scoffed, but not so many as might be expected. On occasions, when I arrived at a party, one of my old crowd has shouted some such thing as "The Reverend will now lead us in prayer!" A remark like this has never failed to produce at least one person who would hunt me up later, ask me a flock of questions, indicating he was looking for an answer to some of the problems in his own life.

Shortly after making my first decision in this way of life, I spent the week-end at a friend's house. During the evening, mention of the Oxford Group was made and it naturally developed I was identified with it. The crowd was a very worldly one; several scathing remarks were passed and the man who shared a room with me was especially cynical. When we retired for the night, I began to wonder what he would say if I got down on my knees to say my prayers. I determined to do it at all costs, and down I got. My thoughts were not on my prayers, however, for all I could think about was—if he opened his mouth, I would jump up and poke him in the jaw. He never said a word.

At one cocktail party the host, who was a newcomer in these parts, was very insistent about my taking a drink.

Finally, in the presence of several guests, he said, "You worry
me by not taking a drink." One of my old friends immediately piped up, "Listen! If he was drinking, then you'd really
have something to worry about!"

During my drinking days, I thought very few people knew
how much I really drank. I have since discovered the world,
at least my small world, could almost tell the number of
drinks I consumed per day. This applied to the new way of
life. People I hardly knew stopped me, said they thought
what had happened to me was wonderful, and wished to
hear how it had occurred.

When I really got my life rearranged, the mess cleared
up, the barriers of envy, hate, greed, and fear removed, and
looked to God for my daily orders, everyone noticed the
change. The blare of trumpets was not necessary (Chap. 20,
153–62).

For years, my father had been a vestryman in an Episcopal church in every town and city where we lived. We
always sat in the second pew from the front. I was dragged
to church every Sunday until about my last year in school,
when I rebelled.

The minister had said something I interpreted as being
socialistic and I took it as an opportunity to go into my act.
How I happened to hear him, I don't know, as I usually
counted the light-bulbs, number of panes in the windows,
etc., hardly knowing when I should be standing, sitting or
kneeling. I leaped with great gusto on his remark, announced
if he ever again mentioned anything I thought was socialistic I would stand right up in church and tell him what I
thought of him. My family, being of dignified variety, were
horrified at the thought their son might do something as bold
as this. I know they must have shuddered internally at the
very idea. Compulsory attendance ended–I went to church
when I pleased, which was very seldom.

During the thirteen years of married life, previous to meeting the Group, I went to church twice—both times on Easter. It meant nothing to me at all. I didn't like the people who went and I was darned sure they didn't like me. The only sermons I could bear were the ones containing funny stories, but as they were clean stories, they only partially pleased my sense of humor.

It seemed to me most church-goers only attended because they were afraid to stay away; they thought God kept a record of this and the number of times they broke the Ten Commandments. After they died, they believed, this record was balanced, and depending on the balance, they went either to heaven or to hell. It all sounded like a lot of poppycock to me; anyone who believed it was a moron, and even if it were true, it was most certainly a speculation what either place would be like. I preferred to do as I damned well pleased here on earth and let the hereafter take care of itself.

None of the people I saw in church appeared to have any answer to their own difficulties. They all acted suppressed, under cover of the cloak of piety. They were just as mean, money-grabbing, selfish, dishonest, and impure as anyone else. In fact, this made them appear worse to me than non-religious people. I felt sorry for the ministers because most of them appeared to be misfits, using the church as a means of livelihood.

Soon after coming in contact with the Group, I started going to church and I have been going ever since. I usually go to the Episcopal Church, as years ago it was in this church I was confirmed. It seemed very natural to return to it; however, in this I am in no way rigid. Recently I attended a Roman Catholic Mass and felt very much at home.

After the change in my life everything connected with the Church took on an entirely new light and meaning. The prayers I had formerly muttered without thinking, now suddenly appeared full of meaning. It was like a wholly new discovery. My attitude toward the minister changed; he became some one for whom I had a responsibility, to whom I owed my support. How could he be helped or helpful, if I was unsympathetic with him and his problems?

At first, I resented the fact the church had been of no assistance when I had been in such need. This feeling disappeared when I realized the majority of ministers were not really surrendered to God and willing to do anything He asked; had not shared their lives and cleared away the debris; in short, were much the same as I had been, except they had tried to do the right thing, whereas I had not even made any effort.

Although I thought churchy people were suppressed, of one thing I have always been positive—in no way was I repressed. If I could not do a thing, at least I talked about it. I always believed I was an outgoing person. Recently, I seriously investigated this part of my make-up. The discoveries were illuminating, as well as startling.

I found I positively reeked of suppressions, most of which were so buried and hidden it took a real excavation to uncover them. They were all problems beyond my power to solve. I poured them in a bottle labeled "Irritants" and endeavored to keep it corked. The cork continually kept popping, with the result that I showed a bad disposition about many other things, when the real cause was in the bottle, hidden away from everyone, including me.

When unearthed and exposed, a strong evil desire can often be used as a constructive force. I had always felt if I wanted to do a certain thing there were only two courses open; I did or did not do it. Now I have discovered if I face the desire and let God take care of it, there is always a third and much more satisfactory way.

Many of my repressions were confused and mixed up with other things which, on the surface, had no bearing on each other. One was my desire to write. I had always been afraid any literary effort would not be applauded—might be ridiculed—so I had always planned to write anonymously. At times I would write, then tear it up, which seemingly relieved the desire.

This wish to be unknown was also mixed up with other feelings. When I was playing any game, if I did not seem to be excelling I would do something which would make onlookers think I was not seriously trying to do my best. Once, in a speed test for jumping-horses, called a time trial, I appeared with a beard and overalls. If I did not do well, everyone would say, "Oh, he's only fooling." Then, as a matter of fact, I rode like hell and did my best to win.

Another tremendous urge was to travel. Very well hidden and so annoying was this irritant, I actually hated to see pictures of foreign countries, because I felt annoyed at not being able to embark immediately. I do not know what this desire means. Since I have faced it, I no longer squelch the thought of other lands, knowing full well God has some use to which He will put this urge.

The desire that my family should be well taken care of, be happy and successful, has brought up the question of just how I loved them. Did I love unselfishly, or did I demand something in return? Did I love them expecting them to be a credit to me, to be outstanding, so people would point them out as being *my* family, or did I love them for themselves? Would I do or say something which would cause them to dislike me, if it were the right thing for them? These were very hard things to face. I saw that my love was a very demanding thing. I expected too much in return for it, was extremely interested in what people said about my family and how it reflected on me.

In addition, there were the million and one desires for this and that, which did not seem to have any answer, but, when faced, cleared the decks and often resulted in the appearance of some very constructive vision.

The answer to suppressions I have seen in my own life is: any desires I may have were given me by God, and constitute a force He wants used for some good purpose. The use He makes of them will satisfy me and will create the things He wants created.

In the past few years an enormous amount has happened in me, to me, and about me. As a result, my family and my business have been greatly changed. Even some friends and acquaintances have been affected.

I have not become absolutely honest, pure, unselfish, and loving—hell, no, nowhere near! But whereas I used to be a drunk—now I do not drink at all; I used to think of no one but myself—now I endeavor to be considered of others; I used to lie when I felt like it—now I try to tell the truth; I used to look down on most people—now I see qualities in them which I never knew existed; I used to be restless and unhappy—now I am calm and happy; I used to think the other fellow was always wrong—now I do not; I used to feel that conditions, times, the town, the state, the country, and the world were at fault and should be changed—now I realize it is individuals like myself who need to be changed. For it is only fair to assume that if *individuals* lead honest and unselfish lives, the *groups* of which they are a part become honest and unselfish, too—with what far-reaching effects on business, domestic, and civic relationships I can safely leave to better imaginations than mine!

In this way of life I am very new. The sample I have tasted is swell—I want more. In seeking and following this new path I do not know where I may go, what I may do, how I may live, or what I may become, but I do know that I have found a formula for my own life which works better than any I have ever known.

Believe me, from where I sit, the future looks fascinating—full of adventure, action, romance, happiness, and tremendous hope (Chap. 21, 163–71).

13

The Way to Find God

Be still, and know that I am God; I will be exalted
among the heathen, I will be exalted in the earth.

Psalm 46:10

"Give in," he cries, "admit that I am God, high over
nations, high over the world."

Psalm 46:10 (Moffatt)

Alcoholics Anonymous, A.A.'s basic text, commences
by spelling out the seemingly hopeless condition of mind,
body, and spirit that plagues the alcoholic. In that book the
"Doctor's Opinion" points out that an alcoholic is restless,
irritable, and discontented until he experiences the ease
and comfort that come with taking a drink. The drink in turn
leads to the spree, trouble, and remorse, followed by yet
another baffling round. In his first book, *Realizing Religion,*
Sam Shoemaker set forth a spiritual solution to what he

151

called "spiritual misery" (or, as A.A.'s text calls it, "spiritual malady"). Shoemaker said that many suffer from being restless and discontented, and that the only remedy is to find God. He said: "What you want is simply a vital religious experience. You need to find God. You need Jesus Christ."[1]

A.A.'s text seems to echo Shoemaker's words: "There is One who has all power—that One is God. May you find Him now!"[2]

Shoemaker's later book *National Awakening* explains how to find God. It contains several ideas that bear resemblance to some of A.A.'s steps.

You are all familiar with the words of the forty-sixth Psalm, "Be still, and know that I am God; I will be exalted among the heathen, I will be exalted in the earth." You have said those words to yourself, sometimes with frantic search for faith, sometimes with strengthening and reassuring comfort, when life was getting to be too much for you. They have called you to recollection, to steadiness, perhaps to inner quietness and the realization of God. They have held before you the promise that God will be revered throughout the world.

But the other day I came across Dr. Moffatt's translation of these words, a modern translation, as you know, and one based upon a far richer scholarship than was possible for the translators of the Authorized Version: though they stand second to none in their use of English. Here is the meaning which Dr. Moffatt finds in these familiar words, "Give in, admit that I am God, high over nations, high over the world."

We have usually taken those words as a soothing introduction to a period of meditation. "Be still, and know that I am God," and they may have served us well. But, "Give in, admit that I am God" is a challenging introduction to religion and to life itself. Soft dilettantes of religion have made the words, "Be still, and know that I am God," an easy lullaby to rock themselves into dreamy reverie and a comfortable state of mind. But nobody can find any lullaby in that imperative, "Give in, admit that I am God." Here is no sentimental God of the spiritual dabbler: here is the majestic God of Reality, speaking in authentic and unmistakable tones to His creature, man. The true note of inspiration, in the Bible and outside it, is that the Word should be clothed with an authority which marks it as coming from beyond. I feel that element strongly in these words. They were given to the writer: he did not make them. God spoke them to him, and he wrote them down.

I believe they are the gateway to a true faith, and show us the way to find God. Let us look at them more closely.

They assume in us a natural capacity for God. It is as if they told us that God is our natural element, as water is for fish. It is unnatural not to believe in Him, not to be in touch with Him. The emptiness, loneliness, homesickness, wistfulness, wonderment which all men feel at some time is a hollow place in the human soul that God is meant to fill. None other can fill it—not human love, nor achievement, nor fame, nor wealth, nor happiness. "Thou has made us for Thyself, and our hearts are restless till they find rest in Thee." Estrangement from God—the condition in which numberless people today find themselves—is an unnatural condition, as the story of the expulsion from Eden clearly shows: it was not God's plan, it came about through human disobedience. We hear Him saying to us, "Give in, admit that God is, and that He is the great Answer to your life, and that your life never is nor will be complete without Him."

But these words also assume in us a natural resistance to God. As a matter of fact, we all both want God and fear to have Him, as Francis Thompson said, "Lest, having Him, I must have naught beside." We want God because He created the hunger within us for Him. We want Him from dependence, from fear, from loneliness, from the craving for perfection in our souls. We want Him from bewilderment, confusion and darkness. We want Him from innate love for Him, from insatiable preoccupation with the invisible Reality of the world. But we do *not* want Him entirely, because of His exactions. The demand that we merely behave ourselves would fall in line with prudent self-interest, but the demand that we be guided by Him in all things is really costly. We do not want the uncertainty, the discipline, the constancy, the humiliation, the openness to His plan which a guided life requires. Everyone is hungry for God, and most people know it. But this resistance to the exactions of God either keeps them away or makes them seek a less costly way to have Him: most of the "fancy religions" are studied devices to imitate the comfort of Christianity while eliminating its Cross. A great many people turn their backs on historic Christianity, not, as they say, because they cannot accept its theology, but because they know it has a moral backbone; because it asks so desperately much of them; because it offers to them only the peace of a battle joined and won, not that of a battle evaded. When a man truly finds God, that resistance is recognized and then relinquished. God is driving directly at this innate resistance in you and me and all mankind when He says, "Give in, admit that I am God."

I see in these words, too, not only the truth of our capacity for God and of our estrangement from Him, but a vigorous emphasis upon God's lordship over every man. God is God, and self is not God–that is the heart of it. It is an actual fact that we become God to ourselves unless we have God to believe in: the final reference becomes ourselves, perhaps ourselves at our highest and best, perhaps ourselves at our most petulant and picayune, but ourselves nonetheless and all the time. Ourselves are, like our bodies, the inevitable instruments through which we live and serve God. Put in their places, they become servants of God; but riding on top of us, they become His rivals. So inescapable are they that sometimes we want to cry out with St. Paul, "Who shall deliver me from this dead body of myself?" And self is often still left when we think we have killed it entirely: we want to become merely passive, merely negative, with a self so utterly yielded as not to exist. But that is not what God wills: He does not wish us to have no wills at all, but continually to conform our wills with His. As Tennyson said in his inspired line, "Our wills are ours, to make them thine." The same self which has resisted God must be the self which freely cooperates with Him. God is speaking directly to our bumptious, assertive, wheedling, insinuating selves: "Give in, admit that *I* am God."

There is decidedly something here, too, for people with intellectual difficulties about religion. He says to them virtually: Begin with the premise of God as a postulate. Take the word "admit" in the sense in which it is used in an argument, where there must be some assumption from which you start. There must always be some initial intellectual toehold, or you cannot discuss anything or arrive at any conclusion. I have seen dozens, and even hundreds, of people come through to a real faith in God through beginning by acting as if He were, assuming that He is, and allowing Him to make Himself known in events and directly. Consider the words "Give in." This does not mean to abandon your intellectual faculties: it means first to begin with the assumption of God. But it means more: it means for intellectual people that they must put aside their pride, their love of standing apart from and above the common run of people who need God and believe in Him, for that can forever destroy the possibilities of faith. It means that the deepest, toughest stumblingblock in the way of faith is not intellectual skepticism, but moral confusion and personal self-will; and the place to take hold may not be the place of immediate intellectual difficulty, but the place of moral independence and self-will. I am convinced that what keeps most people from faith in God is not good reasons for disbelief, but rather wrong ways of approach, unhappy associations with religion of some one type; but, most of all, *pride* in the form of self-sufficiency, intellectual conceit, the lingering picture of ourselves as superior to religious faith. The trouble lies not in an honest mind, but in a dishonest character. To such people God says, "Give in, admit that I am God." And then He discloses Himself as they honestly seek and obey.

Here, too, as we have already suggested, is God's drive on the central citadel of the will. One cannot help comparing it again with the older version. "Be still"–that calls to the emotions. "Know that I am God"–that calls to the mind. But "Give in"–that calls straight to the will. How many people in this fussy, nerve-ridden day repeat the words "Be still" to themselves in fruitless command! We certainly need to be still: a man told me the other day that he had been in a hurry for fifty years. But trying to subdue your feelings is dealing with symptoms: the cause is a will that is not yielded to God. It is not your nerves, your fears, your feelings of futility and frustration, that are fundamental: they have been created by your maladjustment to life, your resistance to God and circumstances, your self-will. In every situation God has a will which He can reveal to you only if you are wholly open to Him. You may now be suffering from the results of taking your own way, and God does not save people from that suffering: He does offer to us all the choice of a better way, of His way, so that in future we may find ourselves on the right road instead of the wrong. It is not a matter of how we feel, nor primarily of what we believe: the crux of all religion is the set of the will Godwards. Real religion has begun for many of us at the moment when we recognize that.

Now, the place where our wills pass out of our own hands and into God's is the place of surrender: and surrender is our answer to this command from God: "Give in." People sometimes say to me that they want to cooperate with God, but they do not see the point of surrendering to Him: one can only reply that they have never yet come face to face with God, they are only toying with the idea of religion; when you face God, you know that He is saying to you "Give in" for the sufficient reason that He is God and deserves the whole gift of ourselves, the whole obedience of our wills. Cooperation will come later–gladder, freer cooperation than ever you knew you could have with God: but it begins with surrender. The wonder of this is that you can begin just where you are. You can find God today and now if only you will be honest. I used to think I should understand Christianity when some day I found a big book with all the questions and all the answers: but it did not come that way. I began understanding it when I "gave in" to God in an act of the will called self-surrender. That is not a matter of how you feel, or even of how you think: it is a matter of how you orient yourself to the ultimate Reality of the universe which is God. Because He is, and because He loves us, He begins with us where we are. We need know little about His nature, or the completeness of His self-revelation in Christ, to make this initial step towards Him. Understanding will come later: what is wanted first is relationship. That begins, as thousands will tell you from experience, at the point where we "give in" to God.

How is it done? A man spoke to me the other day in Calvary House, a member of whose family has had a great spiritual experience. He began by saying: "Do I have to go through one of these great upheavals they talk about? I have tried always to serve God, and been a good influence. I believe if I died tomorrow, I should be accepted by God." And I said to him: "How many more are there who will be accepted because of what you have said to them and been to them? As for influence, may I ask what is your business?" He told me what it was. "Now," I said, "if you sent

out from your company a representative to another city to
do business, and if at the end of two months you asked him
for a report of what had been done, and he told you he had
made a general good name for the company, but nobody
had taken any of his goods to buy, you'd put him in a psy-
chiatric ward. Shouldn't we be at least as efficient in our
work for Christ as in our business?" He saw the common
sense of that, and said he'd like to find an experience of
that sort. I introduced him to another man, with whom he
made the surrender of his life, involving letting God come
into a family row about money, and telling his business
partners that from now on his business life was to be based
on Christ's standards and guidance and he wanted them
to know of this new decision. He took the two crucial
points of his personal and business life, and made their surrender to God the occasion of the total surrender of himself. Upheaval?—yes, a complete personal revolution; but
no emotion and fireworks in it, the whole thing centering
in the giving of his will to God.

And what happens next, so that this one decision becomes
the gateway to permanent living in Christ and building His
Kingdom? First of all, his own continued relation with God
in prayer, and daily waiting on God in quiet. Each morning
that decision is renewed as we "give in" afresh to God, admitting that He has the order and the answer for the day. The
Bible begins to open up to such a person, as he begins to
take hold of it by experience and it brings, not only courage
and illumination and personal inspiration, but teaching
which the Spirit uses to guide our minds into all the full, rich
truth about Christ. There is need for the fellowship of other
people who are living this same way of life in God, and are
able to put that man in touch with others in his own city,
and tell him how to increase their number by his own work.
His family will see the difference in him; so will those business friends, so that spiritual doors will fly open to him

through which he can go with a message of Christ that this generation can understand, a message couched in terms of a life-giving experience. And then he will find himself caught up with the world-wide movement of the Spirit today, and become part of a program of world-changing by life-changing. So that he who came in a problem a few days ago will be himself a worker and a warrior: so that one who needed God to help him in his own needs moves forward to the realization that God needs him to get to many other people.

There are two surrenders for most of us: one where we give ourselves to God to get out of a scrape, and another where we give ourselves to God that He may use us to help the world get out of a scrape. The first surrender is necessary, but will become selfish and die unless it moves on into the second. No man is truly redeemed who does not become part of Christ's whole redemptive process in the world, so that the new life which has come to him may come through him to others. God owns the nations and the world, and His majesty above them is a fact which needs no defense from us. The other day I said to a clergyman in this city that a certain group of people were bringing God back into human life, and he said: "But God is already in human life." I said: "Yes, but what good does it do if people don't know it? These people are making the world know He is there."

Those words come with special force to our whole generation, "Give in, admit that I am God, high over nations, high over the world." For the nations are seeking to work out their own problems and their destinies by themselves, and they are not getting along any too well with it. Pride and self-sufficiency are back of most of our present difficulty. In a silly fear that by mention of religion we shall step on somebody's toes, we give ourselves to man-made programs which leave God out of the picture. We shall get no basic order out of our chaos till we "give in" to God, admit that He is Lord of nations and of ages, and exalt

Him in our national life. That will save us, and nothing else will.

God give us all grace today to still the other voices and influences about us, to look in the one necessary direction, to leave behind us self-sufficiency and pride, to "give in" to Him with all our hearts (NA, 45–54).

14

The Turning Point

Sam Shoemaker often quoted Professor William James. James's principal book enabled Bill Wilson to validate the religious experience that empowered him to recover from alcoholism. Shoemaker frequently quoted or referred to the following words of James: "Self-surrender has always been and always must be regarded as the vital turning-point of the religious life."[1] Just before describing the steps in their program of recovery, the authors of *Alcoholics Anonymous* say: "Half measures availed us nothing. We stood at the turning point. We asked His protection and care with complete abandon."[2] Shoemaker wrote: "Let go! Abandon yourself to Him."[3] The following is a chapter from Shoemaker's *God's Control* that elaborates on the urgency.

Now Is the Time!

One Sunday morning one of the most faithful and loyal men in my parish said to me in the porch of the church, "It has taken two thousand years for us to get as far as we have with Christianity, and I suppose it will take another two thousand before the world is very different." How far do you think that is a statement of objective and inexorable truth, and how far does it represent personal conservatism which itself contributes to the very delay which it deplores? Let us examine the whole problem of pace in religion. Wherein is religion sudden, wherein is it gradual: what place has decision, what place has growth: what must we leave to God's Providence, and where does urgency spur our own responsibility? Does our danger lie in driving ourselves too fast, or in too low a level of expectancy and therefore inadequate action? These are not academic questions: upon our answer to them depends far more than we may realize.

Let us take it, first, in the whole area of getting started in religion ourselves. Some of us have been surrounded by religion all our lives. We do not remember the first words we heard about it or the first impressions we had of it. Our families went to church and were Christian people. We began our religious life, as we like to say, when we began our natural life, and both have been a matter of growth. Now William James once said that there were some people for whom religion was like a "dull habit," and others for whom it was like an "acute fever." If you are satisfied with being of the "dull habit" variety, you may never allow a spiritual crisis to arise in your life. Personally I am not. It is my belief that finding God is a good deal more like falling in love than it is like merely growing up. And falling in love is a matter of exposure: it may grow over a period of years steadily, or it may come in a flash. But when it has come, you know it; you do not ooze into it unconsciously. When Christ said to a very respectable church member named Nicodemus that he needed to be born again, He certainly made it plain that his kind of "dull habit" variety of religion was insufficient: He virtually said to Nicodemus, "You only think you have gotten started: your spiritual life has never begun." I am sure that if He stood face to face with many of us, He would say precisely the same thing.

I fall into the class of those we have described, who have been brought up in a Christian home and family. I began to realize how inadequate was the religion I had, when I saw that I could not give the power of Christ to people who needed it. In the case of a man who later committed suicide, in the case of one who was later fired from his job, in the case of a flier about to go off for action at the front in 1917, in the case of a renegade and brilliant clergyman, I simply failed. "By their fruits ye shall know them," and by my fruits I was wanting. What you can't give, you haven't got. Someone told me to begin by facing honestly my sins, just where I was, and surrendering them to God, together with my will. In one sense you can say that this was a fulfillment of what I had always known; yet it was also something very much more than I had ever known, for next day another person found the same experience. About that time I read William James' *Varieties of Religious Experience*, and found this sentence: "Self-surrender has always been and must always be regarded as the vital turning-point of the religious life." That cleared matters for me. When a life is changed, God acts to forgive and transform a human life: but God can only act as man acts also in full surrender to Him. The question for us to ask ourselves to-day is not, Did I surrender to God long ago? but, Am I surrendered to God now, about everything in my life? Have I moral victory? Have I inward peace? Is there anywhere a strained or broken relationship? Can God change lives through me, and is He doing it now? Unless these things are true, we need to make a true start.

Second, let us think about what true growth in the spiritual life means. We have just been saying that nobody can decide gradually—you can think gradually, you can take a good while for an exposure to be effective: but a decision is always an act. We cannot grow into grace, but we can and must grow *in* grace. How do we do it? Moral growth does not come by "tapering off," it comes by decision. You are not "slowly getting over" any moral defeat by gradually doing better: the only way to win a moral victory is to quit doing what is wrong. One of the surest dangers in the Christian life is the compromise which means to get over a fault or sin "some day." Half the dead Christians in the world are dead because of this. Live ones deal with sin immediately and drastically, and having given it to God, have victory over it. If we are going to win out against any sin, we must say to God and ourselves, "Now is the accepted time!" Part of growth is increasing nearness to Christ. I used to think that this was a mystical state of mind to be sought for its own sake. More and more I see the force of what He said, "If ye love Me, keep My commandments,"—that is, Do the things I tell you to do. Prayer and guidance are always immediate, because God is there when we are open. Last summer a man's life was changed, and guidance came to him at once which changed his home situation. Later he stepped aside from God's control in his life, would not wait on God at all, and lost the experience, which threatened the whole disruption of his home. The other day he came in, faced himself and the situation anew, became open to the truth, and guidance began again coming into his life. He hasn't been growing during that time, except in the sense of finding that life without God gets increasingly difficult: either one is in touch with God, or he is out of touch. "Now is the accepted time" for God's guidance—now or never. Part of growth is a deeper service to others: not only more service, but primarily better service. Now one can grow in experience of the way in which others are helped, and learn by observation and trial what helps them: a life-time is not too long to keep studying the way God deals with people and problems; but you don't need a life-time to begin, you only need definite conviction about your own responsibility. Even when it comes to a deeper perception of the intellectual meaning of Christianity, the knowledge of the Scriptures and the understanding of the faith, these will go on yielding up treasures year after year: but the will to study and to understand, in order to be equipped for spiritual warfare, the will to take the kind of action in which alone intellectual propositions are found valid, is not a matter of long thought, but of determination. Growth, then, is very largely a matter of decision.

Third, the matter of getting other people started in the God-controlled way of life. How long ought that to take? No one can answer that question finally: most people make their decision within a relatively short time, and yet recently a man made his decision with whom some of us have been working quietly for thirteen years. The real question to ask is: Am I surrounding people with the kind of living, information and demonstration which catches their imaginations, and makes them want the thing I believe in? Now the fact is, I think, that the vast majority of so-called Christian people have never seriously considered getting other people started in the God-controlled way of life: they pay us preachers to do it for them—and then they wonder that a force like radicalism, spreading by the sheer impact of one convinced person upon another who is not convinced, moves in on their world and threatens to destroy it. But we are too reticent, too modest, too well-bred to talk about our religion: it is, we say, our "example" that will count in the long run. And so we go on living a life about two degrees better than the life of the world about us; there are still drunkards, and divorces, and nervous break-downs, and misunderstandings, and difficulties with employees, in our families and social acquaintances, as there are elsewhere—and yet we think we are somehow being noble enough to convince people that we have something they have not. The truth is we are fooling ourselves. The forces of evil and subversion work so much faster, so much more cleverly, than we that we are negligible forces in the world. And the real difficulty does not lie in outsiders unconvinced about the value of God and faith: it lies in the stubborn conservatism of those who accept these things theoretically, but have no strategy for winning the world through changed individuals; only a self-made plan for making the world a little better. A man who had been exposed to people who are actually changing others over a period of nearly nine years said to me, "You can't hurry people!" Now that is a straight projection of his own unwillingness to move and change his mind. You can't hurry people to change their minds about something which is inadequate to make them change their minds: but we have got to move faster than we are now moving if we are going to get there in time to make the control of God effective over the control of fear, greed and materialism. All that is really needed to convince people about religion is an adequate experience in your own life, and an adequate demonstration in terms of the solving of some common problem, like business or industry, about which you can speak briefly and intelligently so as to interest a responsible man to-day. That gives him an adequate exposure. If his conservatism or selfishness or something else prevents his taking it at once for himself, move on to someone else: events may be the one thing that will convince him, the kind of events which result from his kind of selfishness. The point for you and me is to be honest with ourselves: are we furnishing a sufficient demonstration and articulation of religion to convince people about us; and do we need to find out what it is in us that prevents us from finding such demonstration and articulation as many others are finding? At that point in the preparation of what I was saying, I talked to a real estate operator in this city who for years has had the idea of more gracious and understanding relations between his clients and himself: but recently God has come into that man's life; and superintendents and employees who smiled at his kindly dreams about better relations, while keeping their own conviction that "business is business," are now seeking to find what it is that has so greatly changed his life, and is actually bringing about better relations. Yes, business is business; but God is also God: and He knows more about business than any man does. These men began getting interested the moment they saw an adequate experience and demonstration. Does that take years to do? "*Now* is the accepted time!"

Finally, what about changing the world? Is our friend right–will it take another two thousand years before the world is very different? The forces of change and movement are in the air, and can be harnessed for God as well as for other ends. It didn't take two thousand years for Communism to capture a sixth of the earth's surface. It didn't take two thousand years for seven men to change the course of events in Germany. Don't forget the quick stroke as well as the slow process in history. Not alone is the oak valuable: you can hear the corn cracking sometimes as it grows up so swiftly, but it is valuable also. I have seen with my own eyes the concrete answer to every problem that can arise on this earth, because men are in touch with the living God and His plan. I have seen that bringing back love and peace to homes from which it was lost. I have seen it lifting from men's lives the burden of fear,–fear of life, fear of death, fear of pain, fear of the future. I have seen it bridging differences of class and race that were called insuperable before. I have seen it bringing co-operation, friendliness and trust in industries where competition, suspicion and self-interest had been the order of the day. I have seen it alter the policy of newspapers, schools, hospitals, prisons. I have seen statesmen find a new idea of God's plan for a country. And I have seen the positive force of God at work in human lives move steadily across the face of whole nations, till public opinion was a different thing, till every area of national life felt the impact of it. These things are facts, not visions. God has the answer. The burden does not lie upon Him to act, but upon us to let Him act through us. When an answer is available, and we delay, we may make the answer too late. The only time I ever saw Major George Haven Putnam was one day in 1923 in his London office: when he said to me with emphasis, "This is my prayer, Give peace *in our time,* O Lord." He was then in his eighties: but his faith and hope were not in the distance, they were concerned with the immediate.

The answer to the problem of pace in religion, the concrete answer of how fast matters ought to go, and how fast we ought to go to keep pace with God's plan, lies with God Himself. We think of God, and then we remember the eternal ages during which His creation moves forward, and then we slump back into a kind of despair and inaction. Do not forget that, while God may take ages to make a coal field, the electricity which is produced from that coal can girdle the earth six times in a second. When you plug in your radio, or your lamp, you get sound and light at once. God's spiritual force is like a vast, unmined coal field. Changed human lives in touch with Him are like generators that turn His force into the heat of human love and feeling, into the light of wisdom and illumination, into the power of consistent spiritual drive. God's force is there. We all know what it will do. A man to-day can still keep his house lit with candles, but the world sees by electric lights. He can refuse to have a radio, but if he will open his mind and his ears he can hear people in China or Australia as clearly as in the next room. A lot of us Christians are still backward. In face of clear evidence of what happens when men tune in on God's broadcast messages, we look back to the past, we say the old is good enough for us—and the result is that many a person not long out of complete spiritual ignorance and indifference goes far beyond us, and is used in the spiritual revolution while we only stand on one side cheering while it proceeds; or perhaps even wondering what it is that is happening. The answer to it all lies in God's guidance. He who makes oaks and corn, coal and electricity, gives both steady growth and swift change.

Look at all the facts honestly—was there ever a time when one could take those words so literally as to-day, " . . . behold, now is the accepted time; now is the day of salvation"? The need is universal, and on all sides is the growing conviction that the only answer is spiritual force. Over against this, the demonstration of the answer: lives lifted above every kind of personal problem, bridges flung between hitherto irreconcilable individuals and groups, spiritual demonstrations of power in offices and factories where before sheer materiality was supreme. As these adequate experiences and demonstrations multiply, new areas are captured, brought under God's control. The only practical question for us is: Am I capturing for God the salient for which I am responsible, my home, my business, my club, my union, my town? If I am not, is the reason that my own experience is inadequate, or unshared; and needs demonstration and articulation? It is not God that is holding things up; nor the slow, inevitable delays of history itself. It is only ourselves.

Let us have done with contentment with a spiritual pace which lags behind God's plan. Let us dare to tell Him that He can make us very different if He wills to. Let us open ourselves to God that He may lay upon us all the urgency that is within His own heart. *Now* is the accepted time (GC, 136–45).

The Meaning of Self-Surrender

The meaning of self-surrender to God is the deepest meaning in all the experience of religion. There is something deep-hidden within us which makes us feel that whatever God is, He is more ideal than we are, and that we shall tend to find our life by yielding it, in as nearly an absolute sense as possible, to the Ideal Power which we call God.

The very earliest stirrings of faith in God carry with them some natural response of this sort. It is hard for us to think of God without thinking also of our duty towards Him, and it is impossible to conceive that duty in any vitally personal sense without the consciousness that we cannot begin to do it until we have first offered the whole of ourselves to God. Like human love, religion is impossible without the maximum of self-giving.

I am perfectly sure that self-surrender is for most people an unrealized aspiration. They feel the edges of it in great moments of joy or of sadness. Music stirs it in them, if they are susceptible to music. Art may do it, or a sunset sky. A great spoken word, or the convincing life of a saint—there are a thousand possible stimuli to the thought of self-surrender to the Power of the universe. But this generally goes off into diffuse ether. The thing is mostly emotion which does not harness itself to something that needs to be done. It is fitful and unsustained. It is a glimpse we get into reality, that does not last long enough to become an abiding possession, a permanent attitude of obedience and trust and loving co-operation.

If I can today, I want to draw this thing out of the vague region where for most of us it resides, only occasionally invading our minds, and put it where it may become actual for us all. May I say to you, frankly and personally, that I was a missionary on foreign soil, with a Christian home, confirmation, many student conferences, and a decision to enter the ministry behind me, before I ever saw the luminous depths, the liberating power, of the experience of self-surrender? My brethren, these things ought not so to be; and it is one of the great resolves of my ministry that they shall not be where, by preaching and talking in season and out of season, upon the reality of the experience, I can prevent them from being. It is a lamentable thing that in our religious instruction, and our preaching, we can hit upon so many peripheral and secondary things, while Christian people go through their lives without knowing that this central experience is possible for them.

William James has told us that people belong to one of two types, the once-born, or the twice-born type. Emerson was a type of the first, a mind always at unity with itself, with little consciousness of duality or division, which holds communion with the Absolute as with a familiar Friend, and which finds harmony and peace by falling naturally into step with the purposes of Providence. The twice-born type is aware of disunity, division, a rift at the center of being, something in oneself that is out of gear and out of step and needs righting. St. Paul is the archetype of it, and the heart of the need for second birth is his cry: "Wretched man that I am! Who shall deliver me from the body of death?" The once-born type takes naturally to goodness and elevated activity which makes for happiness and peace. The twice-born type is beset with anxieties and inward friction which can only find happy activity after an inward readjustment has taken place.

A great many of us belong to the twice-born group, or ought to belong to it, who need to find it out. We like to think we are once-born, and all right as we are. We have glossed over the division and disunity within us by a fictitious outward self-possession and quietness. But the rift can only be fully healed when we have given ourselves over to God.

Now, for this twice-born type, there are two possible ways of surrendering. A surrender may be largely a deliberate act of will. A man having seen the issue of surrender, and knowing that God wants the whole of his life unreservedly, may make the plunge and throw himself utterly upon God to do with as He will. Such a surrender is that described by Prof. Henry B. Wright, of Yale, when he says of a meeting he attended at Northfield: "I was afraid I should be asked to go as a foreign missionary, but I went down. There, seated in an armchair at one end of the room, was the greatest human I have ever known, Dwight L. Moody. He spoke to us simply and briefly about the issues of life, using John 7:17 as his theme: 'If any man willeth to do his will, he shall know of the teaching, whether it be of God, or whether I speak from myself.' There in the quiet, without anyone knowing what was going on, I gave myself to God, my whole mind, heart and body: and I meant it." Those of you who know of Henry Wright's profound influence for more than twenty years upon student life in this country, and the emphasis he always put on the need for absolute surrender to God's will, will not ask whether such an experience is lasting; you will know that it is both lasting and widely multiplying.

I could give you a hundred instances of men and women whom I have known, who have, at a critical place in their lives, made this momentous turning and have never retraced their steps or gone back on their decision. You may be the kind of person who, having seen the choice, must deliberately, coolly, sanely, and with resolve, hand yourself to God by making a deed of trust for your life, disposing of yourself to Him so that you can never take yourself back again.

There are others of this twice-born type who cannot thus take the kingdom of heaven by force. There are two elements in the complete experience of which I speak, if surrender grows into conversion: man's turn, and God's search. For some of us, the critical element is the dedication of our own wills. For others it is the moment of God's invasion. Surrender is, then, not so much effort as is required in throwing ourselves over upon the mercy of God, but only so much effort as is needed to open the door of our life to Him. We must all know that what God does for us in a conversion is the great matter, and not what we do for ourselves: but there are natures in which this is the supreme part, in the sense that surrender is a passive thing rather than an active one. I am not now talking about resignation under pain and trouble, which is quite another question. I am speaking of the need for an open and relaxed and unstruggling mind as the medium through which God can alone come into the lives of some people. Possibly there is an element of each emphasis needed in us all, so that we both make the effort of deliberate self-surrender and also cease from all effort, so that no exertion on our part may interfere with God's dealing with us. We may not be able to tell which is to be our particular means of surrendering until we try it.

One is bound to be asked the question whether it is a relatively sudden matter for many, and a combination of suddenness and gradualness for others. For the person who wakes up to the fact that they are matured in every other way, but babes in their spiritual development, so that the great experience of religion has yet to come, I believe that it is likely to be an experience which takes place at a definite and recognized time. It is significant that James wrote: "Self-surrender has always been and must always be regarded as the vital turning-point of the religious life. . . . One may say that the development of Christianity in inwardness has consisted in little more than the greater and greater emphasis attached to this crisis of self-surrender." Crisis, mark you, not process.

The process which comes before the act of surrender is the long discovery that the way of self is no way at all, and leads nowhither–the lonely, despairing, feverish desire to be rid of oneself. And the process which comes after the act of surrender is the steady matching-up of the actual with the ideal, the rethinking and remoulding of life in accordance with the great decision. Both processes may take time, much time. But the decision itself has the definiteness about it which any decision has: you may prepare long for a decision, you may work long to carry it out. But when you decide, the hammer falls, and there cannot be delay.

Now I want to speak of four immediate results of surrender, when one has wholly let go of one's life, and is living continually with reference to God. By these I think it fair to test whether we have surrendered or not.

The first is a wide sense of liberation. The queer thing about self-will is that it kills the very thing it wants: freedom. If you know any more abject slave than the man or woman who has throughout his life had his own way, I would like to know where you find one. One of my friends tells me, when I talk to him along these lines: "I feel as if you were trying to put a big, black overcoat on me, and button it tight." But it is precisely his own complete control of the issues of his life which is, year after year, buttoning the overcoat tighter and tighter; and it is the very surrender which he fears that alone can bring him liberty. There is no freedom under God's wide heaven like the freedom of having committed yourself, lock, stock, and barrel, to the will of God. The joy of it is an unearthly thing, which follows you and grows greater with the years.

The next result is an enquiry into one's life-plans in the large, to see if they be such as God would choose as His first, best plan for us. For younger people this is bound to concern their life-work and their marriage, and to demand that these great choices be made upon the basis of honest search for God's will. There are in the world a great many empty places, hard places, thrilling places which the world cannot see as thrilling. God wants workers there. There is a lot He wants done in this world, and there are very few who will lay themselves open to His plan, and promise to fit in wherever He says. Here, again, many a man or woman fears he must become a missionary, or give up what promises to be a successful worldly marriage to wait for one with better foundations; and it seems a heavy cross. Yet when one makes the commitment with regard to these large life-plans, he finds that God makes no mistakes, and the thing he thought he could never do may be the very thing he loves to do most.

There is a retroactive element in a genuine surrender, too. You cannot give your life to God without being willing to turn back into the past, and there make right the things you know to have been wrong. Past wrong leaves its roots in our subconscious minds, and if you dig below the soil you will find the old foundations just as they were left. Personal relationships which have been filled with misunderstandings and irritation, business deals which have compromised principle, injustice which calls for the fairness to reopen the question, rudeness or criticism or tale-bearing which only honest apology and confession will make right—these things feel the change in the atmosphere when we have genuinely surrendered, and they must be acclimatized to the new life. Nobody has really given in to God who leaves untouched the unforgiven grudge, or the unrighted wrong. The new life demands a clean slate.

And then there must be growing victory over sin. Deliverance!—that was the cry of victory of Christianity to the first century. St. Paul went into a rotten port-city like Corinth, infested with all the degradation of the worst of Greek degeneracy, and told his people he was determined to know nothing among them but Jesus Christ. Real Christianity has always been able to save men from sin. And when I find people who have all their lives been coming to church, and have never mastered a quick tongue, a disagreeable spirit, the touchiness which resents the slightest interference with one's own desires, and which makes one hard to get along with, I do not say the Christianity has failed, I say that we Christians have simply not surrendered our whole hearts to the Lord Jesus Christ.

For two nights of this past week my work has carried me to the Jerry McAuley Water Street Mission. I heard there the vivid and simple and unostentatious testimonies of men who had been redeemed from all kinds of sin. They said they had been kept for two days, several weeks, twenty years, by the power of Christ. There is a difference between that happy and vivid and unashamed religion, and our decent and reticent and less effective kind: the difference isn't in the amount of decency nearly so much as it is in the amount of power. I would to God the churches of this city had in them the power that is there, that we expected people to be converted as they do, expected them to witness as they do. And back of that power over broken sin there lies a great yielding, a deep surrender to the love and will of God.

Now, my friends, I always want to say a special word in a sermon like this to those whose major choices have been made, and who feel it is now a question of making the best of it because it is too late to change. It is never too late. When you miss God's first best plan for you, He has a second, and if you miss that, a third. Your situation is always new to God. He can and will always begin over again to deal with you, and give you another chance. It is a great thing to surrender to God in the fullness of youth, but it is also a great thing to surrender at any time. I beg you not to think of yourselves as too far along the way to change.

Let us today ask ourselves with complete candor whether we ever have surrendered everything to His will. Did we miss His whole plan for us years ago by taking a turn we knew was wrong?

Have we felt the pressure of His love all these years, and feared to respond to it, as Francis Thompson did, "lest having Him, I should have naught beside"?

Have we given Him our homes, our money, our ambition, our joy, our suffering, our human ties, our characters, our hearts? Is there somewhere a conscious withholding?— for if there is, there is so much less of that freedom and joy and peace in believing which comes alone when we give all.

It is one of the dearest hopes of my life that this congregation will learn the art of winning lives to Jesus Christ: the beginning is with ourselves. No man can give what he does not possess. You cannot ask another to give himself to Christ till you have given yourself. This is no academic self-examination. Something is desperately wrong with our modern version of Christianity, and I suspect that it is the want of just this surrender amongst us. I believe you are in or out. Henry Wright startled some people once by saying: "No man or woman oozes unconsciously into the kingdom of God. In the final analysis, all enlist, and every soldier knows when he enlisted." But I believe he was right. Have you ever enlisted? Or have you all your life hung around the recruiting station, and thought about it? God has a place for you, a work for you to do. You will do it, or it will go undone.

"Who then offereth willingly to consecrate himself this day unto Jehovah?"

Let us pray:

O God our Father, it is so easy for us to drift along, and say our prayers and sing our worship as though with all our hearts we loved to do Thy will. Thou knowest us better than we know ourselves, and in Thy presence we see how much of our life is outside Thy control. Grant us grace to give Thee everything we have and are, and use us for Thy glory. For the sake of Jesus Christ our Lord. Amen (RTW, 43–53).

15

The Three Levels of Life

A person can choose to live on three levels: (1) instinct—
"I want!" (2) conscience—"I ought!" (3) grace—"I am
guided!" In one of his most popular writings, *The Conversion of the Church,* Shoemaker called for the life that is willing to be based on listening for the Voice of God. A regu-
lar part of such a life is a "Quiet Time," consisting of Bible
study, ordinary prayer, and then listening—with the writing
down of the thoughts that come. This, said Shoemaker,
puts common men and women in touch with the living God.
Proverbs 3:6 is one of many verses confirming the fruit of
a God-guided life: "In all thy ways acknowledge him, and
he shall direct thy paths."

I have sometimes said that there are three levels of life on
which men live: the level of instinct, the level of conscience,
and the level of grace. The personal pronouns and verbs
which go with these are, "I want," "I ought," and "I am
guided." The lower level represents the place where we get
what we desire, live as we choose, take what we like. The

179

next level represents the place where we scruple, where we follow duty, where we behave ourselves and obey the law. The third level represents the place where we have gotten above conscience and instinct alike, where desire and duty coincide, where the will of God has become our meat and drink, where we are at the beck and call of the Holy Spirit and where "His service is perfect freedom." I need not remind you that there are a great many Christians who think, not in three levels, but in two: good and evil; and they fit everybody into them. It is easy to know what to do with the fellows who live for the present and the body and this world: they live by instinct. But can we lump the conscientious and the guided all in one? I think not. Saul was as conscientious as he could be, but he was also as wrong as he could be. So were the Pharisees. So are all the legalists from that time onward. So far as I can see, Jesus was just as anxious to get us up from the level of conscience to the level of grace, as He was to get us from the level of instinct to the level of grace.

Where do most of the church-people that you know live—on which storey of this three-storied category? Where is our living? Where is our giving? Most of us, though not all, are above the plane of common instinct. But are we above the plane of common scrupulosity? Where does your minister live? Does he call on guidance, write letters on guidance, preach sermons on guidance, deal with his session of council on guidance, make his personal plans on guidance?—or is he driven to make calls because it is expected of him, does he write because the letters lie on his desk and urge him to answer them, does he preach because it is part of the stint he is paid to produce, does he deal fearfully, high-handedly, obsequiously, unreally, with his laymen's board; does he even have areas where he frankly thinks himself deserving of a little personal indulgence, so that he slips down *two* storeys, and has his drink, or his theatre-night, or his risque story, or his delicious morning grouch every so often?

And where do you lay-people live? Is comfort such a god to you that you are obliged to have just so much of it before you even begin to serve God? Or is money like that? Is food in that class, or travel, or the luxury of an occasional temper? Or have you moved up a class: and has fidelity to religion made you righteous but rigid, made your religion obnoxious to others, made you censorious of people that sin when you do not know how to win them out of it for Christ, made you uncomfortable with them and them with you, made your religion negative, prohibitive, uninteresting, lack-lustre, so that when the children get out from under your wing they say, "No more of that for me"? I am thankful for people who are systematic about their work in the church, on whose presence and faithfulness one can always count. But I always want to tell them that there is yet a third level where they all might live. It includes all that is best in the level of conscience, and it includes one thing which is good in the level of instinct, namely the element of liberty. But it takes the tyranny of the body out of the one, and the tyranny of the conscience out of the other: and lets God's Holy Spirit be the deciding factor in every choice. I am convinced that Jesus lived and died that you and I might live on the upper level of God's grace and guidance. I feel sure that He wanted His whole Church to live there. It is the only thing which will bring back again "the lost radiance of the Christian religion." For that lost radiance is only the glow of authentic inspiration, the outer shining of the inner light.

How, then, shall we seek this inspiration from the Holy Spirit, till His slightest motion is our ready desire? I can only speak from my own experience. Something happened to the quality of my time of prayer when I moved up out of the old conception of a "Morning Watch" (which had a way of slipping round till evening), to the conception of a "Quiet

Time." The emphasis was in a different place. Formerly I had sought to find my way up to God. Now I let Him find His way down to me. Listening became the dominant note. Not the exclusive note: for there was Bible study first, taking a book and studying it straight through; and there was also ordinary prayer, confession, petition, thanksgiving, intercession. But the bulk of the time is listening. Most of us find it indispensable to have a loose-leaf note-book, in which to write down the things which come to us. We find that in trying to remember what has come before, we block what is coming now: we find it impossible to remember sometimes the things which come even in a brief Quiet Time. The Chinese have a saying that "the strongest memory is weaker than the weakest ink." We do not want to forget the slightest thing that God tells us to do: and I have sometimes had a rush of detailed guidance which came almost as fast as I could write it.

It goes without saying that such a period is best in the early morning, while the body and mind are fresh and rested, the perceptions clear and unclouded, and the day is before us. We shall want to stop more than once in the day for further direction, especially with others about problems which concern them and us. But nothing makes up for our private time alone with the living God. There He may give us the conviction of sin that clears us of a stoppage and sends us to someone with restoration and apology. He may send us a verse of encouragement, like "Fear not," "Go in thy might, have not I sent thee?", "All is well." He may warn us against a wrong course, or a tedious and time-killing person, or a tendency in ourselves. He may send us to the telephone to call someone—or tell us to write a letter, or pay a visit, or take some exercise, or read a book. Nothing which concerns our lives is alien to His interest, or to the doing of His will. He may give us guidance about how to help someone, to tell us what is the matter with them or us. For growing hundreds of people, this has become a simple, effectual way by which the daily will of God as to the common decisions of our lives may be both sought and found. And the final test of it all remains the unity, the joy, the spiritual power of the lives of people who maintain this practice.

Some may say that they can see how this would increase the devotional life: but what has it to do with helping the Church to take the world for Christ?

Now if I am sure of one thing, I am sure of this: it is the absence of the note of personal inspiration, of the availability of the resources of Almighty God, for the humblest person about the smallest question—it is the reduction of Christianity, instead, to a sterile and self-generated goodness, which has brought the average man to-day to believe that the religion of Jesus Christ means trying to live up to the moral ideals of Jesus by human will-power, sometimes fortified by prayer. That is not only characteristic of the view of religion outside the Church, but inside as well. Religion to-day is largely the imitation of an example, when it ought to be the hearing of a Voice. And so the interior life of Christians has become a dynamo, busy with plans and philanthropies and activity; when it ought to be a receiving-set, primarily concerned with catching the messages from on high. The preaching of the churches has become largely a dry appeal to the human conscience, a call to be good, instead of a watering of the soil of the inner life in the certainty that when men are in touch with the living God they will of course be good: one is weary of the finger of conscience being taken as the symbol of religion. The leadership of the Church has become a marshalling of the already over-taxed energies of men and women, into very worthy social service; instead of being concerned to replenish their waning supply of interior energy, quietness and light. We have backed down from our original position that men must be born anew into the world of the Spirit, and live out their lives from a centre of divine inspiration: we now take the people we find as we find them, line them up in service, send them out to help their fellows with cheer, friendliness or money, because they are too inwardly poor to help others with joy, fellowship and the gift of a spiritual experience. These things are well enough for those who act from humanitarian motives: but they are red herrings across the trail of the Christian Church when they are made the substitutes for, instead of part of the fruits of, Christian experience. The ordinary man has only time for the main business of religion: he wants to know whether you can put him in touch with the living God. For a time he may call all this activity "practical," but in the long run he will see that it is unpractical and steals the time and energies of Christian ministers and workers from the main matter, and long to have us come back to first things. When religion has run the gamut of substitutes and chimeras, when the layman has been put off by everything from theology to amusements, he comes round to the one thing in religion that matters most: a real hold on God, and a real knowledge of His will by genuine revelation. I have seen not a few hard, selfish, worldly men whose first interest in true religion was aroused through the suggestion that it is possible to be in touch with the living God through guidance. We have tried pretty nearly everything else. Maybe we shall succeed by offering to this generation a working supernaturalism, free of theoretical controversy, filled with practical clarity and direction and energy.

The crux of Christianity to-day lies most certainly in the supernatural. Whether Christianity be a true revelation of God's Self to us in His Son and in His Holy Spirit; or whether it be another human effort to explain the riddle of existence, and to be as decent as we can in a fundamentally mysterious and perhaps meaningless universe, taking Jesus as the one small candle in an infinite darkness–that is the real issue. One regrets unspeakably that this profound question has been so acrimoniously dealt with, and upon such purely intellectual grounds, by differing schools of thought.

Perhaps in an age when science has made experimentation cogent and congenial to us, we shall better demonstrate the supernatural than prove it. I could introduce you to many scores of rather typical modern people who, a few years ago, would have told you they had no faith whatever in the supernatural, but who to-day live by the light which they believe comes to them direct from God. Some of these people have been through the whole mill of psychology, with its tendency to make one distrust personal experience and almost to analyse it out of countenance: but still they believe that in the phenomena of the guided life they are dealing with something which definitely comes from God to us, something which has no parallel whatever in any of the self-influencing forces of the human mind. Where these people go, a kind of spiritual glamour goes with them which has nothing to do with their human personalities. Where they gather, you will find the happiest and most vital human society that I know. And you will find them continually exercising such influence upon other people as would convince the most skeptical that there courses through them a Power not themselves.

If these God-guided personalities, these common men and women in touch with the living God, could be multiplied upon a wide scale; if the churches could be filled with them, and the world could find it out, we should soon have the world turning back again to the Church, because of the simple fascination of the God-guided life. For while the generation in which we live has been bred to intellectual objections about religion, that generation has already begun seriously to question the gains of the past few decades, with war, selfishness, famine, depression and an epidemic of suicide, as the concomitants of unbelief, godlessness, paganism, self-will and sin. We are beginning to see the connection. We are beginning to wonder whether faith may not be the one indispensable factor in a world which shall be decent enough to live in. We have seen how certain modern trends of religion have petered out, and how religion has been betrayed by some of its own backers. I have a conviction that the next development in religion will lie in a revival of personal religious experience, with the emphasis upon conversion, upon God's guidance, and upon the infection of the social order through personalities who are in touch with God. Humanitarianism in religion has failed us.

God give us back the inspiration of His Holy Spirit (CC, 59–67)!

16

What the Church Has to Learn from Alcoholics Anonymous

God chose what is foolish in the world to shame the
wise, God chose what is weak in the world to shame
the strong. . . .

1 Corinthians 1:27

During the weekend of the Fourth of July past [1955], I
attended one of the most remarkable conventions I ever
expect to attend. It was a gathering in St. Louis of about five
thousand members of the movement called Alcoholics
Anonymous. The occasion was the celebration of their twentieth anniversary, and the turning over freely and volun-
tarily of the management and destiny of that great movement by the founders and "old-timers" to a board which
represents the fellowship as a whole.[1]

As I lived and moved among these men and women for three days, I was moved as I have seldom been moved in my life. It happens that I have watched the unfolding of this movement with more than usual interest, for its real founder and guiding spirit, Bill W., found his initial spiritual answer at Calvary Church in New York, when I was rector there, in 1935. Having met two men, unmistakable alcoholics, who had found release from their difficulty, he was moved to seek out the same answer for himself. But he went further. Being of a foraging and inquiring mind, he began to think there was some general law operating here, which could be made to work, not in two men's lives only, but in two thousand or two million. He set to work to find out what it was. He consulted psychiatrists, doctors, clergy and recovered alcoholics to discover what it was.

The first actual group was not in New York, but in Akron, Ohio. Bill was spending a weekend there in a hotel. The crowd was moving towards the bar. He was lonely and felt danger assailing him. He consulted the church-directory in the hotel lobby, and found the name of a local clergyman and his church. He called him on the telephone and said, "I am an alcoholic down here at the hotel. The going is a little hard just now. Have you anybody you think I might meet and talk to?" He gave him the name of a woman who belonged to one of the great tire-manufacturing families. He called her, she invited him out at once and said she had a man she wanted to have meet him. While he was on his way, she called Dr. Bob S. and his wife, Anne. Dr. Bob said he'd give her five minutes. He stayed five hours and told Bill, "You're the only man I've ever seen with the answer to alcoholism." They invited Bill over from the hotel to stay at their house. And there was begun, twenty years ago, the first actual Alcoholics Anonymous group.

The number of them now is beyond count. Some say there are 160,000 to 200,000 recovered alcoholics [1 million now], but nobody knows how many extend beyond this into the fringes of the unknown. They say that each alcoholic holds within the orbit of his problem an average of fourteen persons who are affected by it. This means that conservatively two and a half million people's lives [14 million now] are different because of the existence of Alcoholics Anonymous. There is hardly a city or town or even hamlet now where you cannot find a group, strong and well-knit, or struggling in its infancy. Prof. Austin McCormick, of Berkeley, California, former Commissioner of Correction in the city of New York, who was also with us at the St. Louis Convention, said once in my hearing that A.A. may "prove to be one of the greatest movements of all time." That was years ago. Subsequent facts support his prophecy.

On the Sunday morning of the convention, I was asked to talk to them, together with Fr. Edward Dowling S. J., a wonderful Roman Catholic priest who has done notable service for A.A. in interpreting it to his people, and Dr. Jim S., a most remarkable colored physician of Washington, on the spiritual aspects of the A.A. program. They are very generous to non-alcoholics, but I should have preferred that it be a bona fide alcoholic that did the speaking.

In the course of what I said to them, I remarked that I thought it had been wise for A.A. to confine its activity to alcoholics. But, I added, "I think we may see an effect of A.A. on medicine, on psychiatry, on correction, on the ever-present problem of human nature; and not least on the Church. A.A. indirectly derived much of its inspiration from the Church. Now perhaps the time has come for the Church to be re-awakened and re-vitalized by those insights and practices found in A.A."

I think some of you may be a little horrified at this suggestion. I fear you will be saying to yourself, "What have we, who have always been decent people, to learn from a lot of reconstructed drunks?" And perhaps you may thereby reveal to yourself how very far you are from the spirit of Christ and the Gospel, and how very much in need of precisely the kind of check-up that may come to us from A.A. If I need a text for what I say to you, there is one ready at hand in 1 Corinthians 1:26, ". . . God chose what is foolish in the world to shame the wise, God chose what is weak in the world to shame the strong." I need not remind you that there is a good deal of sarcasm in that verse; because it must be evident that anything God can use is neither foolish nor weak, and that if we consider ourselves wise and strong, we may need to go to school to those we have called foolish and weak.

The first thing I think the Church needs to learn from A.A. is that **nobody gets anywhere till he recognizes a clearly-defined need** (emphasis added). These people do not come to A.A. to get made a little better. They do not come because the best people are doing it. They come because they are desperate. They are not ladies and gentlemen looking for a religion, they are utterly desperate men and women in search of redemption. Without what A.A. gives, death stares them in the face. With what A.A. gives them, there is life and hope. There are not a dozen ways, there are not two ways, there is one way; and they find it, or perish. A.A.'s each and all have a definite, desperate need. They have the need, and they are ready to tell somebody what it is if they see the least chance that it can be met.

Is there anything as definite for you or me, who may happen not to be alcoholics? If there is, I am sure that it lies in the realm of our conscious withholding of the truth about ourselves from God and from one another, by pretending that we are already good Christians. Let me here quote a member of A.A. who has written a most amazing book: his name is Jerome Ellison, and the book is *Report to the Creator*. In this (p. 210) he says, "The relief of being accepted can never be known by one who never thought himself unaccepted. I hear of 'good Christian men and women' belonging to 'fine old church families.' There were no good Christians in the first church, only sinners. Peter never let himself or his hearers forget his betrayal in the hour the cock crew. James, stung by the memory of his years of stubborn resistance, warned the church families. Today the last place where one can be candid about one's faults is in church. In a bar, yes, in a church, no. I know, I've tried both places." Let that sting you and me just as it should, and make us miserable with our church Pharisaism till we see it is just as definite and just as hideous as anybody's drunkenness can ever be, and a great deal more dangerous.

The second thing the Church needs to learn from A.A. is that **men are redeemed in a life-changing fellowship** (emphasis added). A.A. does not expect to let anybody who comes in stay as he is. They know he is in need and must have help. They live for nothing else but to extend and keep extending that help. Like the Church, they did not begin in glorious Gothic structures, but in houses or caves in the earth, wherever they could get a foot-hold, meet people, and gather. It never occurs to an A.A. that it is enough for him to sit down and polish his spiritual nails all by himself, or spend a couple of minutes praying each day all by himself. His soul gets kept in order by trying to help other people get their souls in order, with the help of God. At once a new person takes his place in this redeeming, life-changing fellowship. He may be changed today, and out working tomorrow—no long, senseless delays about giving away what he has got. He's ready to give the little he has the moment it comes to him. The fellowship that redeemed him will wither and die unless he and others like him get in and keep that fellowship moving and growing by reaching others. Recently I heard an A.A. say that he could stay away from his Veteran's meeting, his Legion, or his Church, and nobody would notice it. But if he stayed away from his A.A. meeting, his telephone would begin to ring the next day!

"A life-changing fellowship" sounds like a description of the Church. It is of the ideal Church. But the actual? Not one in a hundred is like this. The laymen say this is the minister's job, and the ministers say it is the evangelist's job, and everybody finds a rationalized excuse for not doing what every Christian ought to be doing, i.e., bringing other people into the redeeming, life-changing fellowship.

The third thing the Church needs to learn from A.A. is **the necessity for definite personal dealing with people** (emphasis added). A.A.'s know all the stock excuses–they've used them themselves and heard them a hundred times. All the blame put on someone else–my temperament is different–I've tried it and it doesn't work for me–I'm not really so bad, I just slip a little sometimes. They've heard them all, and know them for the rationalized pack of lies they are. They constitute, taken together, the Gospel of Hell and Failure. I've heard them laboring with one another, now patient as a mother, now savage as a prize-fighter, now careful in explanation, now pounding in a heavy personal challenge, but always knowing the desperate needs and the sure answer.

Are we in the Church like that? Have you ever been drastically dealt with by anybody? Have you ever dared to be drastic in love with anybody? We are so official, so polite, so ready to accept ourselves and each other at face value. I went for years before ever I met a man that dared get at my real needs, create a situation in which I could be honest with him, and hold me to a specific Christian commitment and decision. One can find kindness and even good advice in the Church. That is not all men need. They need to be helped to face themselves as they really are. The A.A. people see themselves as they are. I think many of us in the Church see ourselves as we should like to appear to others, not as we are before God. We need drastic personal dealing and challenge. Who is ready and trained to give it to us? How many of us have ever taken a "fearless moral inventory" of ourselves, and dared make the depth of our need known to any other human being? This gets at the pride which is the hindrance and sticking-point for so many of us, and which, for most of us in the Church, has never been recognized, let alone faced or dealt with.

The fourth thing the Church needs to learn from A.A. is **the necessity for a real change of heart, a true conversion** (emphasis added). As we come Sunday after Sunday, year after year, we are supposed to be in a process of transformation. Are we? The A.A.'s are. At each meeting there are people seeking and in conscious need. Everybody is pulling for the people who speak, and looking for more insight and help. They are pushed by their need. They are pulled by the inspiration of others who are growing. They are a society of the "before and after," with a clear line between the old life and the new. This is not the difference between sinfulness and perfection, but it is the difference between accepted wrong-doing and the genuine beginning of a new way of life.

How about us? Again I quote Jerome Ellison, in his report to God (p. 205): ". . . I began to see that many of the parishioners did not really want to find You, because finding You would change them from their habitual ways, and they did not want to endure the pain of change. . . . For our churchmen like crimes of bland, impenetrable pose, I offer shame. . . ." I suppose that the sheer visibility of the alcoholic problem creates a kind of enforced honesty; but surely if we are exposed again and again to God, to Christ, to the Cross, there should be a breaking down of our pride and unwillingness to change. We should know by now that this unwillingness, multiplied by thousands and tens of thousands, is what is the matter with the Church, and what keeps it from being what God means it to be on earth. The change must begin somewhere. We know it ought to begin in us.

One of the greatest things the Church should learn from A.A. is **the need people have for an exposure to living Christian experience.** In thousands of places, alcoholics (and others) can go and hear recovered alcoholics speak about their experiences and watch the process of new life and outlook take place before their eyes. There you have it, the need and the answer to the need, right before your eyes. They say that their public relations are based, not on promotion, but on attraction. This attraction begins when you see people with problems like your own, hear them speaking freely of the answers they are finding, and realize that such honesty and such change is exactly what you need yourself.

No ordinary service of worship in the Church can possibly do this. We need to supplement what we do now by the establishment of informal companies where people who are spiritually seeking can see how faith takes hold in other lives, how the characteristically Christian experience comes to them. Some churches are doing this, but not nearly enough of them. One I know where on Sunday evenings laymen and women speak simply about what has happened to them spiritually; it is drawing many more by attraction. This needs to be multiplied by the tens of thousands, and the church itself awakened.

As I looked out over the crowd of five thousand in Kiel Auditorium in St. Louis, I said to myself, "Would that the Church were like this—ordinary men and women with great need who have found a great Answer, and do not hesitate to make it known wherever they can—a trained army of enthusiastic, humble, human workers whose efforts make life a different thing for other people."

Let us ask God to forgive our blindness and laziness and complacency, and through these re-made people to learn our need for honesty, for conversion, for fellowship and for honest witness!

17

What Is Conversion?

If you want a comprehensive scientific definition of conversion, William James has given us a good one: "The process, gradual or sudden, by which a self, hitherto divided and consciously wrong, inferior, and unhappy, becomes unified, consciously right, superior, and happy." That will bear rereading and study. Harold Begbie puts it more categorically and simply when he says, "Conversion is the only means by which a radically bad person can be changed into a radically good person." It is thus a breach, a breaking off, a turning, a change. It is a period put to the past which we reject, and an entrance into a new life which we adopt with enthusiasm.

The gloomy old writer of Ecclesiastes was a glorious poet and an inveterate pessimist. He says some very skeptical things about human life which make his spirit seem closely parallel to that of the modern materialist. In one place he laments, "That which is crooked cannot be made straight."

Here is the word of the militarist who says that war is "inevitable"; of the practical person who allows some compromise with principle as necessary in getting on; of the large number of persons who think filthy jails and punishment the best we can do for criminals. This is pessimism *par excellence*. Everyone rejects it who has any faith in the future of mankind.

But do we so decisively reject it as regards ourselves? Do we not rather quietly assume that we have done about all the fundamental changing that is possible for us, in spite of what "crooked" there may be left in us? How large a majority of those who pray week after week, "that we may ever hereafter serve and please Thee in newness of life," or "that we may hereafter live a godly righteous, and sober life," go home irritable and selfish still, keep up some worldly habit, settle back in defiance of greater aspirations, accept again the terrible old binding conventions—too spineless to do "something loving and something daring"—and then come and pray likewise the next week? Henry Churchill King tells us that "we develop power or character not by general striving, not by resolving in general, but only by definite, concrete applications in definite relations. . . . General self-denial and general surrender to God which involve no particulars are fruitless enough." And while in the slums religion is constantly regenerating markedly evil characters, in the churches and in that large group of religious people outside them, the fact that we are not changing proclaims loudly that, whatever religion can do for roughs, actually it does very little to improve radically its more constant devotees.

What does this mean? It does not mean that religion is any the less able to save conventionally decent people, but it means that our particular kinds of sins are peculiarly insidious, peculiarly inaccessible to the regenerating influence of religion. It means that we are as badly in need of conversion, perhaps, as the wife-beater and the thief—only we are not so much aware of it, and so we are not in a frame of mind where conversion can get at us. Augustine was converted from a life of open shamelessness, and so was Jerry McAuley. But John Ruskin, surely, was ever free from debauchery; yet he felt the need of conversion, and experienced it. And Francis of Assisi, contrary to common opinion, was not, I believe, licentious, but was converted from what seems like a rather bad case of loving to have a good time.

Now the ability to change people is the unique possession of religion. Compared with the amount of regeneration achieved by merely human effort and influence, it is infinite; there is vastly more of it, and it has more to make it last. Ethical teaching may accomplish something, or may more often not, as you will hear from many a weary Confucianist, sated with precepts and longing for power. (And it is only fair to take a thoroughgoing ethical system to judge of its success or its failure; in America we are so set round with the unconscious influences of Christianity that we may produce some characters apparently by ethics alone which owe more than they know to religion.) It is the great assurance of religion that God will always give the regeneration we want if only we put ourselves where we can receive it. When people realize sin, they *want* change—how much nobody can ever tell until he has "been there," or tried to help someone who has. No matter how long the habit has lasted, religion insists that it can be broken. No matter how warped and twisted the nature, Christianity insists that something beautiful will bloom in the sunshine of God. No matter how many years you have sat dull of hearing and lifeless in your pew, really dead spiritually, God has a great spiritual experience and destiny to which He calls you, if only you will rise up to receive it.

You may be thinking that conversion is after all not much of an event, can be psychologically explained, usually comes to more or less emotional people, and is not quite scientific enough for today. I quote Begbie again: "However science may explain the psychological side of conversion, however convincingly it may show that religion is a clumsy term for describing emotional excitement, science itself cannot and does not save the lost and rescue the abandoned. Science cannot do this; it knows how it is done, and yet cannot itself do the thing which it assures us is not a miracle; and science does not do it, does not desire to do it, for the very reason that it lacks the religious impulse which alone can accomplish the miracle." No one can read his "Twice-Born Men," or the many instances of conversion cited by James in his "Varieties of Religious Experience," with an open mind, and doubt that conversion is a spiritual phenomenon as real as any fact that science ever established. Probably if we recoil from the idea of *our* being converted, it is due to doubt whether religion can save "a quite decent chap like me," a feeling that we are in some way superior to the need of it, or else a frank fear of consequences. Conversion partakes of a rather unconventional and unexpected side of life—vital, first-hand religion may refuse to run on worn tracks. And "religion is a fairly unpredictable affair once it gets going." But we need converting all the same. And, as for being above it, perhaps we need not fear to find ourselves in the company of Paul and Augustine and Ruskin and Tolstoi!

Tolstoi's account of his conversion is simple and moving:

One day in early spring time I was alone in the forest listening to the woodland sounds, and thinking only of one thing, the same of which I had constantly thought for two years—I was again seeking for a God. I said to myself, "Very good, there is no God, there is none with a reality apart from my own imaginings, none as real as my own life—there is none such. Nothing, no miracles can prove there is, for miracles exist in my own unreasonable imagination." And then I asked myself, "But my idea of the God whom I seek, whence comes it?" And again at this thought arose the joyous billows of life. All round me seemed to revive, to have new meaning.

My joy, though, did not last long. Reason continued its work. "The idea of God is not God. The idea is what goes on within myself . . . it is not what I seek, something without which life could not be." Then again all seemed to die around and within me, and again I wished to kill myself. After this I began to retrace the process which had gone on within myself, the hundred times repeated discouragement and revival. I remembered that I had lived only when I believed in a God. As it was before, so it was now; I had only to know God, and I lived; I had only to forget Him, not to believe in Him, and I died. What was this discouragement and revival? I do not live when I lose faith in the existence of a God; I should long ago have killed myself, if I had not had a dim hope of finding Him. I really live only when I am conscious of Him and seek Him. "What more then do I seek?" A voice seemed to cry within me, "This is He, He without whom there is no life. To know God and to live are one. God is life. Live to seek God, and life will not be without God." And stronger than ever rose up life within and around me, and the light that then shone never left me again.

We are told that conversion is "gradual or sudden." Augustine was finally converted by a verse in the Bible, and Saul by a vision. Moody said he could almost throw a stone from Tremont Temple, Boston, to the spot where he was converted. Such seem the most vivid, tangible conversions. But there are other kinds as true. I once heard Dr. W. E. Orchard, in London, say that in the providence of God he had had a sudden conversion, and he hoped he would not be misunderstood if he said that ever since he had been getting over it—not getting over the conversion, of course, but getting over the idea that it had all been done then and there, once and for all. The process may be the commoner way; and if it means a constant search for new truth which is at once appropriated and lived by, and not a waiting for things to take their own course, it may also be the safer way.

But one cannot help feeling that the sudden enters into the gradual. Some of us cannot point to a day nor place where conversion took place, and to this extent—if we are indeed converted at all—we can say that it was gradual. But most of us can remember certain occasions which mark distinct progress, when an illuminating truth has been yielded to and made our own, when certain victories stand out, or perhaps one big, hard-won surrender of all to Him. To this extent it has been sudden. And what with ups and downs, some such hybrid as this may be what most of us should expect.

But can one have a conversion at will? And what must we do to have it? Well, we must want it with all our hearts and put ourselves in the way of it. God on His part has longed to win us for years. It has been we who have been unwilling. We must open ourselves to Him, and be prepared to accept all that it will mean to be a child of God. "We cannot, indeed," declares Dr. McComb, "command the great experience, but we can supply the conditions on which the experience will inevitably be ours."

What, then, are the conditions? First, we have got to be willing to break finally with sin. It is not so much this slip or that which wrecks people's lives by destroying their wills; it is accepting evils and wrongs in themselves as inevitable, and giving up the fight. In this there can be no possible reservation or interpretation: we must embark upon the tremendous business of cleansing ourselves, through the grace of God, from top to bottom. And what the sum total of this means, together with the absolutely yielded will, is best expressed in the old idea of self-surrender to God.

Surrender of the whole self to God means the complete dedication, by deliberate act of the will, of one's entire personality to doing the will of God so far as one can discover it. Many will find this idea nebulous, and declare it meaningless; but this is because they are viewing it abstractly, and not in the concrete. Apply it definitely to the things in life that have got to stop, or to the things that ought to come in to replace them; consider that it has the most definite implications as to the way a young person will choose his life work, that the spirit of one's household might have to be radically changed were this surrender once made, that it involves nothing less than the Christianization of our lives and all the lives that we touch, and I think it will lose any marks of indistinctness. It will mean absolute revolution of life for most people who experience it. It is a step taken in the full possession of one's freedom to act, and is a gift of oneself to God, as definite as though one handed to another man a book or a dollar which he never expected to receive again.

William James speaks with great emphasis upon this crisis of self-surrender. He says that it is "the throwing of our conscious selves on the mercy of powers which, whatever they may be, are more ideal than we are actually, and make for our redemption. . . . Self-surrender has always been and always must be regarded as the vital turning-point of the religious life, so far as the religious life is spiritual and no affair of outer works and ritual and sacraments. One may say that the whole development of Christianity in inwardness has consisted in little more than the greater and greater emphasis attached to this crisis of self-surrender."

And this is primarily the business of the will. I believe that not nearly enough has been said of the place of sheer will power in conversion—taking the Kingdom of Heaven by force. It takes will power to thrust out sin with one heave, even for a moment, and let God have place. It takes will power to accept a life-principle as exacting as that of the Gospel and to make its truth an experience instead of an intellectual conviction of which we approve, or with which we are in sympathy. It takes will to believe any change really possible in us, especially if we are along in life, and to cling to that faith in spite of falling once or twice as people often do after conversion. This thought that conversion is, on our part, a matter-of-fact contract, that we have a part in it and work for it and that it hardly ever can come against our will, may clarify and even dignify the idea to many minds. I wish to say emphatically that, while there are often profound emotional concomitants to conversion, as often it is as cool-headed and deliberate as signing a business contract. We need not strain for heights of great feeling; nor need we be afraid that our decision is invalidated if we find our hearts beating faster than usual, or we experience a few moments of ecstasy. These are the periphery–the gift of ourselves is the essential thing.

Given, then, this readiness to yield, the open mind ("empty," as a Chinese boy well put it), the hungering soul, the penitent heart, the surrendered will, the attitude of expectation, and the sense of abysmal need, the whole life given in earnest prayer–what then? This is the highest point thus far in your soul's history. You and God are reconciled the moment you surrender. You know it. The shackles fall away. Self recedes, God looms up. Self-will seems the blackest sin of all, rebellion against God the only hell. The peace that passes understanding steals over you. By power from above, you are "unified, consciously right, superior, and happy."

This impartation of Himself to us is God's part in conversion. It is infinitely the greater part. I have emphasized man's part, because the idea has got lodged in the minds of most people that one must sit about waiting for God to arouse one by some miraculous manifestation, and I believe that we need to realize again that putting ourselves in position is a necessary condition in the great majority of cases. But when this is done, we have done our uttermost, and can do no more. Our part is to ask, to seek, to knock. His part is to answer, to come, to open. In ways which we have not guessed, He has been drawing us "with bands of love." "No man can come to me except the Father . . . draw him." He will not coerce, but He expects from us the final effort of dedication. He has had His part in it all along, ever since those first quivers of dissatisfaction in which our turning to Him began. But, by one of the mysteries of life, He has made it necessary that we should come freely, of our own wills, even while lovingly He has been exerting His irresistible pressure. Then begins the miracle, and the inflowing of that divine grace without which spiritual living is simply impossible. "His saving of men is a personal negotiation between the individual and Himself—that or nothing—and the only infallibility that we need recognize is His voice as each man or woman hears it."

The testimony to the reality of such experiences as these is abundant. I shall quote from Adolphe Monod's account of his conversion:

> I saw that to expect to put a stop to this disorder by my reason or my will, which were themselves diseased, would be like a blind man who should pretend to correct one of his eyes by the aid of the other equally blind. I had then no resources save in *some influence from without*. I remembered the promise of the Holy Ghost, and what the positive declarations of the Gospel had never succeeded in bringing home to me I learned at last from necessity, and believed for the first time in my life, in this promise, in the only sense in which it answered the needs of my soul, in that, namely, of a real, external, supernatural action, capable of giving thoughts and taking them away from me, and exerted on me by a God as truly Master of my heart as He is of the rest of nature. Renouncing, then, all merit, all strength, abandoning all my personal resources, I went home and prayed as I never yet prayed in my life. A new interior life began for me. . . . Hope had entered into my heart and, once entered on the path, the God of Jesus Christ, to whom I had then learned to give myself up, little by little did the rest.

Hear my friend's account, after weeks of restless searching and dark rebellion: "Prayer strove with sin in me, and for the time sin conquered. . . . Yesterday afternoon alone here I fought out my fight, faced realities as I had not faced them for long, and saw what they meant to me, what place they held in my life. Then I went into my room, and–wonder upon wonders–really prayed–found, I believe I can say honestly (now after twenty-four hours have elapsed while I have lived in the radiance of that moment), for the first time Christ the Saviour talking to me, present, receiving me. *Can* it be so? And as I prayed the thought came to me, as if Christ had spoken, that all my doubts of the actuality of religious facts could be laid aside in the reality of the *relation* to Christ. I realized suddenly that I might be a disciple, as real as the Twelve had been; even now that Christ as the Master, the Spirit of His mastership, still lives on earth, and Him I can follow today and here! This sounds simple to you, and is–but oh, it was a wonderful discovery to me! Christ as the Master leads me, and it is in His service that all things must be done, every act touched a little with the radiance of His glory."

My friend had a sudden experience. And too much cannot be made of these moments of illumination and transfiguration.

Tasks in hours of insight willed
May be in hours of gloom fulfilled.

You ask me if it is a real conversion. And I say that it all depends upon what my friend does with it from now on, whether it is a real conversion or not. It has begun well. Dr. John R. Mott said to a group of university men who had entered upon the Christian life the evening previous, "I am not concerned this morning as to how you feel; what I am interested in is what you are going to do." Conversions last when, by the means God gives, we make them last. And finally, the "real witness of the Spirit to the second birth is to be found only in the disposition of the genuine child of God, the permanently patient heart, the love of self eradicated" (RR, 22–35).

18

Those Twelve Steps As I Understand Them

D r. Samuel Shoemaker, the widely known Episcopal clergyman who helped so greatly in the founding of A.A., wrote
this article for the *Grapevine* several months ago. It was
already in type and scheduled for the present issue [Jan.
1964] when the news of his death on Thursday, October
31, 1963, reached us. . . . Here he reviews our Twelve Steps
with that wonderful clarity which has always characterized
his speaking and writing.

One of my most treasured possessions is a pair of gold
discs which I carry daily in my pocket, attached to my watch
chain. One is marked "From the Manhattan group of A.A."
which was given me by Bill when I left New York in 1952;
and the other is marked "Honorary Member in Perpetuity

of Pittsburgh A.A.," given me when I left that city in 1962.
They mark one of the happiest and most privileged relationships I have ever enjoyed. I watched the first beginnings
of A.A. always with interest, sometimes with misgivings
proven false by all that has happened. I thank God for A.A.
and pray daily for all its leaders and members. One of my
most cherished memories is of one of the girls at St. Louis
who said to me, "Dr. Sam, you may not be an alcoholic, but
by God you certainly do talk like one!"

I have always been interested, not alone in what A.A. is
doing for the alcoholic, but in what this program can mean
to anyone who wrestles with a real problem. And who does
not? A pile of wisdom and experience is packed into the
Twelve Steps. I have even compared the inspired forty minutes during which those Steps were given to the Founder,
to the Ten Tables of the Law that were given to Moses on
Mt. Sinai. Many skeptical folk are inclined to say, concerning Moses' inspiration, "O, this is a gathering together
of previous experience; it didn't come all at once like that."
I have no doubt about the previous experience entering in;
but I know that there are inspired hours when people have
been able to gather and put down compendia of truth in a
fashion that can only be called "inspiration." It is an hour
when men's powers are at high pitch and tension, and when
the Spirit of God hovers near, making suggestions. I doubt
if the Twelve Steps that have changed the course of existence for so many thousands of lives could have been the
mere product of human insight and observation. And they
can and will bless anyone, alcoholic or not, who will follow
them through and be obedient to them. They are morally
and spiritually and psychologically and practically as sound
as can be.

1. We admitted we were powerless over alcohol . . . that
our lives had become unmanageable.

The reason so many people in A.A. give thanks that they
are alcoholics is that the problem of living, and the failure
to meet life successfully, is singled down for them to the

problem of alcohol. It is definite and specific. This is exactly what Christianity has taught from the beginning, not only about a problem like alcoholism, but about the whole range of human defeat: that the old cliches like "exerting more will power" are utterly impractical. We are just as powerless by ourselves over temper, or a bad tongue, or a moody disposition, or a habit of lust, or a hard and critical spirit. It is only pride and lack of insight into ourselves that would keep anyone from saying, no matter what their problems or lack of them, "our lives have become unmanageable." This is the first step, not only towards sobriety, but towards self-understanding and the knowledge of life.

2. Came to believe that a Power greater than ourselves could restore us to sanity.

How come? By standing in the middle of the field, calling out to some nameless Power? By reading long books of philosophy or theology? No! By seeing scores, and maybe hundreds and then thousands, of individual men and women whose lives had been defeated and wretched (making thousands more wretched also) transformed into new men and women. Each one of these lives is a kind of miracle—not to be explained in purely human terms. Doctors and psychiatrists and clergy, helpful as they have been to some alcoholics, have no opportunity to report such a high percentage of victories as A.A. How wise A.A. was not to attempt too specific a theological definition! Too fine-spun words were bound to offend some and put off others; nobody can fight against the rather vague term "Power greater than ourselves." The crucible of laymen working it out among themselves, sharing experiences with one another.

3. Made a decision to turn our will and our lives over to the care of God, as we understood Him.

William James, in a classic passage of the "Varieties of Religious Experience," said that the crisis of self-surrender has always been and must always be regarded as the vital turning-point of the religious life. Look through the life of any saint, almost any great servant of mankind, and you will find a moment, an hour, a day when the crisis took place. You can gather materials for a decision over months and years, and you can carry out the effects of a decision over long periods of time, but a decision is sudden. It is a crisis. This is a vivid way of saying that all spiritual experience must begin decisively if it is going to begin at all. This is the great, open, spiritual secret which so many have missed. They tried to ooze into it. You can ooze into booze, but you can't ooze out of it. You can't ooze into God. Everybody in the world needs to learn this truth. I had been a nominal Christian for ten years before anybody challenged me to surrender myself to God. This has to be done more than once, as we shall find; but it has to begin somewhere. This decision puts us in touch with God, so that He can work. It is like screwing the bulb in tight enough to touch the place where the current comes out; but this decision of the will is not the current itself. The current is the spiritual power that flows when we cry out our need to God and He answers.

4. Made a searching and fearless moral inventory of ourselves.

There is no more difficult thing in the world than to face yourself as you really are. We flee from one sin after another as they catch up with us, making excuses all the time, and pleading that our virtues in another direction more than make up for them. What most people need, what all must have if they are to find an answer, is just the willingness to make a searching and fearless moral inventory of themselves. Some sins are obvious. But when it comes to the spiritual sins—like pride, and unforgivingness, and resentment, and touchiness, and inflexibility about having our own way—they are *not* so obvious because their damage is less easy to see quickly. The Ten Commandments will form a good guide. So will the Sermon on the Mount. We may need to sit down with someone who knows us and will be honest with us and ask them to give us a good going over; for most of us are terribly blind and terribly self-deceived. One can even make a "formal confession" to a priest in the Church and not really get wise to oneself. Deepest of all, greatest of all, and subtlest of all, will be *pride* in some form, usually masquerading over the guise of some virtue. Alcoholism may force such an honesty about oneself; would that all the other and more respectable sins did the same thing!

5. Admitted to God, to ourselves, and to another human being the exact nature of our wrongs.

The practice of Confession is, of course, an old one and in some churches a constant one. I suspect that its efficacy depends in part on the sincerity with which the confession is made, and on whether the person confessing really means to get out on new ground and be different thereafter. True confession not only cleans up the past with God's forgiveness, it looks to a new kind of future, else it is bogus. Confession to other lay-people has generally been discouraged by the church as being risky, but A.A. has proved its efficacy in the case of alcoholics, it being possible to take for granted some degree of maturity in the one who hears the story, and some discretion in the keeping of confidences. Let's face it—a certain desperation underlies this. Every minister wishes he could induce the same kind of desperation in the general run of his people, so that they would face their over-all spiritual ineffectiveness and their need to make the same kind of "admission" as alcoholics find necessary. This is always a costly and painful process. I suspect that one reason why it is so effective is that what happens is not only the opening to another human being of the "exact nature of our wrongs," but the laying of pride in the dust by letting someone else know the depth and desperation of our need. Shams go off when you do this. You can't keep on faking. This, and not only the detail of misdoings, is what gets us where we can begin to be different.

6. Were entirely ready to have God remove all these defects of character.

It's not hard to feel like that on a "morning after," but we know this may be remorse and not repentance, superinduced more by a heavy head than by a contrite heart. The further away we get from the last binge of alcohol (or of temper, or whatever), the better the wrongdoing looks—more innocent, more attractive. Are we ready *then* to "have God remove these defects of character"? It is one thing to want to put behind us the inconveniences of wrong-doing, but another to leave behind the wrong-doing itself. This requires two things, I think: (1) a real vision of how much better the new life really is than the old, fortified by what we have heard from people living in it, and (2) real help from the Higher Power, for the will alone is not capable of sustaining this attitude. It is good to be pushed by the danger and hell of the old life, but we must also be pulled by the constant vision of life integrated under God, living in and for and by Him and in and for other people. This is why fellowship is so essential, why it is so dangerous for anyone to think he can take a little spiritual inspiration or power and go off and enjoy it all by himself. Soon or late he is back in the old groove. We need God and we need each other. God alone can give us this new mind and keep us in it. All people need it, so-called good people as well as so-called bad ones. We need to pray for this fundamental willingness to have God change us.

7. Humbly asked Him to remove our shortcomings.

How often have we prayed for "things," or favoring circumstances, or a hundred and one things that were really selfish in nature? Here is where real prayer begins—not ends—in asking God to *change me*. "Lord, I'm not much. You aren't getting much of a prize. It's mostly broken pieces I'm giving you. But I ask You to mend them. You can take the pride and the lust and the anxiousness and the fear and the resentment. Please do take them, and me with them."

Something like that. We may say this in the quiet of our own rooms, or we may say it kneeling in our church, or we may say it as we pray with another person. There must be an intended finality as we make such a prayer. We can't do it with tongue in cheek. So far as it is possible, we mean to be done with the offending thing. We find again that "willpower" only goes far enough to secure our intention: the actual praying of such a prayer already implies help from Him to Whom we pray. Sins get entangled deep within us, as some roots of a tree, and do not easily come loose. We need help, Grace, the lift of a kind of divine derrick. The amazing thing is that such a prayer is answered if we truly want it to be. Our own wills are so much a needed part of this that it almost looks as if we had done it; but the help from God is so much a needed part of it that we are sure that without Him we could not possibly have done it. We learn great truths, long known and often discovered, as we begin a genuine spiritual awakening.

8. Made a list of all persons we had harmed and became willing to make amends to them all.

In some ways it is easier to straighten things out with God than with other people. He fully understands everything, we can count on His forgiveness, we talk to Him as it were "in private." But it is not enough to be right with Him, we must also be right with man. How well do I remember that from the first moment of fresh conviction there was a letter I had to write to someone in the family towards whom I held a long-standing resentment. It was one of the first things I had to do after my decision. You see, we want to get *clear*, to begin anew, to start life all over again. This Step calls for *definiteness*, and it calls for *willingness:* "made a list," and "became willing." How many strained and broken human relationships drag on through years, unresolved, unhealed, unmended. Nobody will make the break and say the two great words of renewal, "I'm sorry." We are willing to tell God, we are not willing to tell man, of our repentance and desire for new life. This can hold us back at the first, and it can trip us way down the line. The laws governing human relations are as iron-clad as those that uphold the stars. Individualize the persons whom we have wronged, and those who have wronged us. Don't forget the wise adage, that "it is harder to forgive those whom we have wronged than those who have wronged us." Get willing to go to them in honesty and humility. It may be the hardest thing you ever did in your life, but it will be one of the most rewarding. We shall need to do it in the beginning of our new life; we shall have to do it, perhaps often, in the after-stages of it.

9. Made direct amends to such people wherever possible, except when to do so would injure them or others.

We must be willing to be absolutely honest, but indiscriminate "absolute honesty" would blow the roof off many a house and destroy entirely some human relations. We must hold nothing back through deceit or pride; we may need to hold something back by discretion and consideration of others. Take a thing like infidelity in marriage; sometimes this must be disclosed to wife or husband in all candor. Sometimes, as in the case of someone with a bad heart, or terribly sensitive or innocent of nature, "telling all" may be almost a self-indulgence for ourselves. The people we have hurt may be dead, in which case prayer to God to let them know our repentance may be all we can do. Or there may be facts in the situation which would help clear the relation, but they involve telling what we know about someone else's sin. This is allowable under only the rarest circumstances: usually it spreads the evil and does more harm than good. If in order to clear our own souls we must damage the reputation of another, it is an extremely dubious practice. Those who deal much with human souls—priests, psychiatrists, lay-folk like A.A.s—must learn the secret of a tight lip, or we shall do damage and gain the reputation of a gossip, which will shut off people's confidence from us. Such actions are usually those of the Pharisee-type, the good and righteous type. But they are sometimes those of the changed Prodigal also—and nothing is worse than the fury of a Prodigal-turned-Pharisee. What is known in confidence should be kept in confidence until or unless the person involved gives us permission to speak of it.

10. Continued to take personal inventory and when we were wrong promptly admitted it.

This is one of the hardest steps in the Twelve. Many of us get steamed up to be completely honest with God, ourselves and some other person at the outset: this points the wisdom of continuing this all the rest of the way. We like to think we have grown past this and are well on the road, but none of us ever gets finally past it. We shall find that when we seek God's help and guidance on some problem, we may need to be open *first* to conviction of sin—then direction. This is part of what keeps the whole thing fresh and contemporary and alive. I am convinced that pride is the root-sin. It is not only, in moral theology, the first of the "seven deadly sins," it is by so much the most serious of them that it is as if it stood apart from the rest as being of a different quality. Pride gets right into our spiritual victories. It insinuates itself into all our achievements, all our successes, even when we attribute them to God, unless we keep open to facing ourselves afresh and making things right where they have gone wrong.

11. Sought through prayer and meditation to improve our conscious contact with God as we understood Him, praying only for knowledge of His will for us and the power to carry that out.

After we see daylight on the conquest of such a clear-cut problem as alcohol—or fear, or resentment, or pride—and feel we are at least making progress, we need a great, overall purpose and motivation upon which to center our growth. Prayer, we shall increasingly find, is not asking God for something we want, it is really asking Him for something He wants. The best of all prayers is, "Lord, what wilt thou have me do?" (Acts 22:10). Prayer does not seek to change God's will, but to find it.

12. Having had a spiritual awakening as the result of these steps, we tried to carry this message to alcoholics, and to practice these principles in all our affairs.

This principle applies to all who have known a great before-and-after experience of spiritual rebirth. Two things are involved in the Twelfth Step: the spread of the awakening to others, and the deepening and continuation of the awakening in ourselves. This was surely the secret of the Twelve Apostles and all the early Christian disciples. J. B. Phillips says they kept to their main purpose of bringing people to God through Christ, and "were not permitted to enjoy any fascinating side-tracks." I should say unhesitatingly that the success of A.A. lies in the readiness of its members to go to any trouble to help other alcoholics, and that when this readiness cools, it is a danger signal. There was an old phrase that used to be current and which contains a great germ of spiritual truth: *Out of Self into God into Others*. Herein is spiritual wisdom and health. We have had to look deep within, probe, burrow, struggle, and in a sense this never stops. But now we must begin to look wide without, concern ourselves with individuals, causes, communities and the wider world. Here is the secret of growth and of spread—not for alcoholics only, but for all.

I often say and shall always say that the Twelve Steps are one of the very great summaries and organic collections of spiritual truth known to history. They have an almost universal relevance (not a relevance alone for alcoholics). They will offer a "way out" for many a person who knows nothing personally of alcoholism. They will point up "the way" for those who have known it and lost it. Thank God for the Twelve Steps and for a man wise enough and open enough to God and to the observation of human experience to receive these truths, and transmit them to the world!

Afterword

On December 5, 1961, the East Liberty A.A. Group, in Pittsburgh, Pa., which holds its meeting at the Calvary Episcopal Church, had a banquet in honor of Dr. Sam Shoemaker. Dr. Sam was retiring from active ministry at this church. The banquet was a sell-out. The principal speaker was Red D., from Talbot City, Md. The following message from Bill W. was read:

"The streams of understanding and love that were gathered together by God in 1935 to create A.A. will always be the source of our infinite wonder, inspiration and gratitude.

"Some may say, 'But Sam is not a stream, he is just a great man!' But we of A.A. know better. We know that he is both. More than twenty-five years ago, he channeled to the few of us who then saw and heard him, the message, the understanding, the loving concern, and therefore the Grace that enabled our small band and all the countless thousands who followed afterward to walk in the Consciousness of God—to live and to love again, as never before.

"On this memorable occasion, we of A.A. want Sam to

know, as perhaps he has never known, the depth of our affection and of our eternal thanks that our Master did appoint him to minister to us when A.A. was very young and, with unsurpassed devotion, ever since."[1]

In memory of Dr. Sam by Bill

On Thursday, October 31, 1963, Dr. Sam Shoemaker, the great Episcopal clergyman and first friend of A.A., passed from our sight and hearing. He was one of those few without whose ministrations A.A. could never have been born in the first place—nor prospered since.

From his teaching, Dr. Bob and I absorbed most of the principles that were later embodied in the Twelve Steps of A.A. Our ideas of self-examination, acknowledgment of character defects, restitution for harms done and working with others came straight from Sam. Therefore he gave to us the concrete knowledge of what we could do about our illness; he passed to us the spiritual keys by which so many of us have since been liberated.

We who in A.A.'s early time were privileged to fall under the spell of his inspiration can never be the same again.[2]

We shall bless Sam's memory forever.

The Twelve Steps

1. We admitted we were powerless over alcohol–that our lives had become unmanageable.
2. Came to believe that a Power greater than ourselves could restore us to sanity.
3. Made a decision to turn our will and our lives over to the care of God, as we understood Him.
4. Made a searching and fearless moral inventory of ourselves.
5. Admitted to God, to ourselves, and to another human being the exact nature of our wrongs.
6. Were entirely ready to have God remove all these defects of character.
7. Humbly asked Him to remove our shortcomings.
8. Made a list of all persons we had harmed and became willing to make amends to them all.
9. Made direct amends to such people wherever possible, except when to do so would injure them or others.
10. Continued to take personal inventory and when we were wrong promptly admitted it.
11. Sought through prayer and meditation to improve our conscious contact with God as we understood Him, praying only for knowledge of His will for us and the power to carry that out.
12. Having had a spiritual awakening as the result of these steps, we tried to carry this message to alcoholics, and to practice these principles in all our affairs.

The Twelve Steps reprinted with permission of A.A. World Services, Inc., New York, New York.

Books by
Dr. Samuel Moor
Shoemaker

Realizing Religion. New York: Association Press, 1921.

A Young Man's View of the Ministry. New York: Association Press, 1923.

Children of the Second Birth. New York: Fleming H. Revell, 1927.

Religion That Works. New York: Fleming H. Revell, 1928.

Twice-born Ministers. New York: Fleming H. Revell, 1929.

If I Be Lifted Up. New York: Fleming H. Revell, 1931.

The Conversion of the Church. New York: Fleming H. Revell, 1932.

Christ's Words from the Cross. New York: Fleming H. Revell, 1933.

The Gospel According to You. New York: Fleming H. Revell, 1934.

Calvary Church Yesterday and Today. New York: Fleming H. Revell, 1936.

National Awakening. New York: Harper & Row, 1936.

The Church Can Save the World. New York: Harper & Brothers, 1938.

God's Control. New York: Fleming H. Revell, 1939.

Confident Faith. New York: Fleming H. Revell, 1939.

Notes

Introduction

1. *Alcoholics Anonymous Comes of Age* (New York: Alcoholics Anonymous World Services, Inc., 1957), 261.

2. *A.A. Comes of Age*, 39.

3. Bill Wilson, *The Language of the Heart* (New York: The A.A. Grapevine, Inc., 1988), 298.

4. Letter from Bill Wilson to Sam Shoemaker, April 23, 1963, a copy of which Dick B. inspected at Bill's home at Stepping Stones during his August 1992 research visit there.

5. *Alcoholics Anonymous*, 3d ed. (New York: Alcoholics Anonymous World Services, Inc., 1976), xvi.

6. *The Co-Founders of Alcoholics Anonymous. Biographical Sketches, Their Last Major Talks* (New York: Alcoholics Anonymous World Services, Inc., 1972, 1975), 7.

7. *Co-Founders*, p. 10.

8. See Bob Smith and Sue Smith Windows, *Children of the Healer* (Park Ridge, Illinois: Parkside Publishing Corporation, 1992), 29, 43, 132.

9. Ernest Kurtz, *Not-God*, expanded ed. (Center City, Minnesota: Hazelden, 1991), 32, 40; *Pass It On* (New York: Alcoholics Anonymous World Services, Inc., 1984), 147; *DR.*

BOB and the Good Oldtimers (New York: Alcoholics Anonymous World Services, Inc., 1980), 71–72.

10. Dennis C., an A.A. historian in Connecticut, informed Dick B. in a personal interview in August of 1992 that John R., an Akron oldtimer, had stated in writing and in a taped interview that Anne read her workbook to alcoholics and their wives at the Smith home when the people came there for what was called "spiritual pablum."

11. See Dick B., *Anne Smith's Spiritual Workbook* (Corte Madera, Calif.: Good Book Publishing Company, 1992), 13–14.

12. *Co-Founders*, 7.

13. Letter from Samuel M. Shoemaker to H. H. Brown, March 13, 1952, a copy of which Dick B. inspected at Bill's home at Stepping Stones in Bedford Hills, New York, during his August 1992 research visit there.

14. Letter from Samuel M. Shoemaker to William G. Wilson, August 5, 1953, a copy of which Dick B. inspected during his August 1992 research visit to Bill's home at Stepping Stones.

15. See reprint of the sermon in Samuel Shoemaker, *And Thy Neighbor* (Waco, Tex.: Word Books, 1967), 24–25.

16. *And Thy Neighbor*, 26–30.

17. See the seven principles of the Bible that Day had written at the request of Shoemaker. Harris included them in his book, *The Breeze of the Spirit* (New York: The Seabury Press, 1978), 18–21.

18. In his interviews with life-time Oxford Group member, Jim Newton, Dick B. learned that the members of the "business team" in the New York area, almost all of whom are mentioned in accounts by or about Bill, included the Oxford Group-Calvary Church vestrymen, Rowland Hazard, F. Shepard Cornell, Hanford Twitchell, and others who figured in Oxford Group writings, such as Victor Kitchen, Charles Clapp, Jr., and Professor Philip Marshall Brown.

19. See Dick B., *The Oxford Group & Alcoholics Anonymous* (Seattle: Glen Abbey Books, 1992), 101–103.

Chapter 12: Shoemaker Touches the Life of an Alcoholic

1. Charles Clapp, Jr., *The Big Bender* (New York: Harper & Brothers, 1938).

Chapter 13: The Way to Find God

1. Samuel M. Shoemaker, *Realizing Religion* (New York: Association Press, 1923), 9.
2. *Alcoholics Anonymous,* 3d ed. (New York: Alcoholics Anonymous World Services, Inc., 1976), 59.

Chapter 14: The Turning Point

1. Shoemaker, *Religion That Works*, 48.
2. *Alcoholics Anonymous,* 59.
3. Shoemaker, *Religion That Works*, 19.

Chapter 16: What the Church Has to Learn from Alcoholics Anonymous

1. This chapter taken from Sam Shoemaker, . . . *And Thy Neighbor,* arranged by Cecile Cox Offill (Waco: Word Books, 1967), 23–31.

Afterword

1. *A.A. Exchange Bulletin* 7:192 (New York: G.S.O. of A.A.): 1.
2. *A.A. Grapevine* 20 (January 1964): 2.